Personal Bible Study Notebook

REVISED

John C. Souter

This special Billy Graham Evangelistic Association
edition is published with permission from the author
John C. Souter.

Personal Bible Study Notebook: Revised
© 1991 John C. Souter

HARVEST HOUSE PUBLISHERS
Eugene, Oregon 97402

Contents

1
The Importance of the Bible

Who but God could have written a book over a period of 2,000 years, in three different languages, on three continents, by at least 37 individual authors, in 66 parts, and come up with the most significant book in history? The Bible is not merely *a* book, it is *the* Book which by the importance of its subjects, the wideness of its range, and the majesty of its Author stands as high above all other books as heaven is above the earth.

Although the Bible is thousands of years old, when it touches on medical or scientific concepts, it deals with incredible accuracy. Technology has a tough time keeping up with this book. In 1861 the French Academy of Science listed 51 facts that contradicted some statement of Scripture. Since then, all 51 of those "facts" have been disproved by science itself.

Bible translator J.B. Phillips wrote that he was "continually struck by the living quality" of the New Testament material he was translating. Often he felt "like an electrician rewiring an ancient house without being able to turn the mains off." The Bible is capable of convicting us, revealing what is good and evil in our hearts. It does this so effectively because it is alive; it is constantly active on God's behalf.

No other book has inspired so much music, so many poems, or such great works of art. No other book has transformed so many lives. It is able to correct, uplift, and feed us. But most important, it alone contains the message of how we can live forever.

Unfortunately, as great and important as the Bible is, it is also the most *unread* book in history. It graces more shelves and gathers more dust than any other book. Why? Because most people simply don't have any idea how to study it for themselves.

The *Personal Bible Study Notebook* is a tool designed to help you dig into God's Word on your own. It was created for people like you, who would love to study the Bible by themselves, but you just don't know where to begin. This notebook contains everything you need to develop a deep, meaningful, and consistent Bible study. Here are some of the things this book can do for you:

- Provide over a year's worth of Bible studies.
- Give you 14 different ways to approach the Bible.
- Offer daily variety.
- Help you record what you learn for future reference.
- Introduce you to every part of Scripture.
- Teach you both Bible facts and principles.
- Challenge you to find the deeper meaning.
- Help you measure your daily Bible study consistency.

2
Why Study the Bible?

In the last century, gold brought the forty-niners to California in search of quick riches. But in a very short time, the rivers and streams no longer yielded the easy nuggets; those who really wanted gold had to start digging beneath the earth's surface.

So it is with the Bible. Many are content to take the simple truths that are easy to find (often depending upon the study of others), but those willing to follow the vein into the mountainside are the ones who end up with the greatest riches.

We live in a day of convenient markets, fast food, and instant oil changes. Fortunes are often made by helping people get some product in a more efficient way. We've been programmed to want things fast and easy, but when it comes to the Bible, the study *process* is as important as what we receive. God wants to build a deeper relationship with us, and what better way than by daily spending time in His Word?

When you consider what the Bible offers in spiritual treasure, can you afford not to learn how to study this book of books? Once you experience how easy and how incredibly rewarding personal Bible study is, you'll be hooked for life.

The Lord tells us to abide in, chew up, observe, feed on, delight in, look intently at, meditate on, and love His Word. In the last days He says, "I will put my laws in their hearts, and I will write them on their minds" (Hebrews 10:16b). But He can only do that if we spend time in His Word, making it our meditation day and night.

As you study the Bible, you will find that the excitement increases; it does not diminish. President Woodrow Wilson commented on this: "Every time you open it, some old text that you have read a score of times suddenly beams with a new meaning." You never have to worry about reaching bottom with this book. There will always be more treasures hidden just out of sight.

Sir Walter Scott wrote, "The most learned, acute, and diligent student cannot, in the longest life, obtain an entire knowledge of [the Bible]. The more deeply he works the mine, the richer and more abundant he finds the ore; new light continually beams from this source of heavenly knowledge."

You will never regret learning to study the Bible. The ability to open this book and discover what God wants to give personally to you will transform your life.

3
Make a Bible Study Commitment

For your Bible study time to be effective, it must be consistent. To be consistent, you must be committed to making that study period a high priority. Determine in your heart that you will set a regular daily time to open and study God's Word.

Each day you will give God at least five minutes. Don't worry about committing yourself to larger blocks of time (you'll find it difficult to stop at just five minutes anyway); the secret to your success will be in making *and keeping* that five-minute engagement with God. So stop, right now, and make that commitment to yourself and to the Lord.

Now, *when* will you study? It is important to think of this study time, not as something you would like to do, but as a definite *appointment with God*. When will it be? It will be much easier to follow through if you establish a definite time slot as part of your regular daily routine.

Some people can concentrate better in the morning while others are evening people. Choose the best time for your study period. And because weekend routines are different, you may need to schedule a new time period for Saturdays and Sundays.

Now, *where* will you study? Again, it is important that you have a specific place you can go where you won't be interrupted. If possible, use the same place every day. You might want to take the telephone off the hook; and, if you're at home, inform your family that you'll be busy during this period.

Each Bible study method in this book gives an (average) length of time that the method should take. Depending upon your needs and your available time, select a method with an appropriate length for each study hour. On weekends, when you have more time, you might want to take on some of the more extensive studies.

There will be days when you don't feel like studying or when you will be running late. When this happens, choose a short five-minute method. Missing one day makes it that much easier to get out of the habit and miss the next.

Each day as you begin to study, record the method you are using or the Scripture passage you are examining. In this way you will be able to measure your daily consistency. God wants us to be faithful, but we'll never be faithful to study His Word unless we have a *plan*. Fail to plan and we're planning to fail. So clearly establish in your own heart that you are *committed* to studying the Bible every day.

4
Understanding the Bible

As you begin to study the Bible, it will greatly help you if you understand some basic facts about this book. These facts will become a framework upon which you can place all the information you receive from God's Word as you study it.

Types of Bible Passages

It is important to remember that the Bible is a collection of 66 books, each written by a human writer to a specific audience at a particular time in history. Each book must be understood in its own context, but it will also help you to understand what its basic purpose is. There are six major types of Bible passages, each with a specific overall purpose:

The Law—The books of the law (Genesis through Deuteronomy) were written by Moses to establish God's dealings with the nation of Israel. They lay out the foundation of Judaism, the civil laws for the nation of Israel, and chronicle the early history of the nation.

History Books—The history books tell the story of Israel's becoming a nation. They officially begin at Joshua and move through Esther (although Genesis, Exodus and Numbers also contain large amounts of historical material). While these books chronicle Israel's story, they also reveal God's ongoing preparation of the world for the coming of His Messiah, Jesus Christ.

Poetry Books—There are five poetry books in the Old Testament (Job through Song of Solomon). Hebrew poetry is unlike English poetry in that it does not rhyme. These books compose the literature of early Israel.

Prophecy Books—The prophecy books predict Israel's future and that of the world. They announced that the Messiah would be coming to suffer and deliver Israel. The prophecy books are Isaiah through Malachi in the Old Testament and

Revelation in the New Testament. It is important to note that almost all Bible books have some prophecy in them.

The Gospels—These four books (Matthew through John) tell the story of the life and teachings of Jesus Christ. They form a quadraphonic image of God's Son, Savior of the world.

The Epistles—The rest of the New Testament is composed of epistles, or letters, written by the early church leaders to churches and individuals. These books form the core of all Christian teaching.

Major Old Testament Events

To understand the Bible it is important to know of several major Old Testament events which have a bearing on everything else in the Bible:

Creation—(Genesis 1:1-27)—The creation of the world, more specifically man's creation in God's image, sets the foundation for all other Bible teachings. It establishes the fact that man is a moral being with a soul (unlike the animals) and is therefore under obligation to his Maker.

The Fall—(Genesis 3:1-19)—When man fell into sin in the Garden of Eden, he inherited a sinful nature and was placed under the curse. The rest of the Bible is God performing His plan to bring man salvation.

The Flood—(Genesis 6:12-13, 18; 8:20-22)—This great cataclysm demonstrated how God sees sin and became a powerful illustration of the future for all unforgiven sinners. Here God also promised to keep the world working properly until the final judgment.

Abraham's Covenant—(Genesis 12:1-3)—God chose Abraham to be the recipient of His blessings. His descendants are promised the land of Palestine; the world will be blessed through his seed (the Messiah).

Israel's Covenant—(Genesis 35:10-12)—Jacob's name was changed to Israel and he received the promise that his descendants would produce a great nation, making the Jews God's chosen people.

The Law Instituted—(Exodus 19:1-8)—The Israelites agreed to place themselves under the law of God and to abide by it. Of course, they were unable to fulfill that commitment. God used this law to point men to the salvation He would be providing in Jesus Christ.

David's Throne—(2 Samuel 7:12-13,16)—God chose David, a man after His own heart, to be the founder of a dynasty without end. The Messiah would come to sit on his throne.

Major New Testament Events

Birth of Christ—(Matthew 1:18-25)—Jesus' birth marks the beginning of God's personal invasion into this world. The fact that He was virgin born is all the more proof that He is God.

Death of Christ—(John 19:17-42)—Christ's historical crucifixion and death is extremely significant because the Bible teaches that He died in place of all mankind, on our behalf.

Resurrection of Christ—(John 20; Matthew 28)—The historical fact of Jesus' resurrection is the foundation for the message of Christianity. It proves that He was God and also brings us the promise that He will one day raise all believers from death.

Birth of the Church—(Acts 2)—The beginning of the church establishes that God ordained and empowered her to minister to the world.

The Second Coming—(Revelation 19)—This event, which is predicted throughout the Bible, is the final outcome of much of Bible prophecy. It is the promise of this event that Christians are to anticipate and be ready for.

Major Teachings

Sin—Knowing about the doctrine of man's sin is central to understanding how God deals with mankind. Sin is the problem that God solved for us. The Bible details man's response to God's remedy in Christ.

Repentance—Repentance is a change of direction away from our sin towards God. Forgiveness for sin is impossible without godly repentance.

Salvation—Salvation from sin to God is the purpose of the Bible. There is no other way to be saved from sin except through Jesus Christ.

Grace—Grace is God's unmerited favor offered to man. In His mercy, God doesn't give us what we deserve (hell) for our sin; instead He gives us what we don't deserve (heaven).

Deity of Jesus—Because Jesus is God, He is able to purchase for us salvation on the cross. If He was not God, His death becomes nothing more than a martyr's.

Inspiration of Scripture—The Bible comes down to us as a divinely inspired (God-breathed) book profitable for teaching, conviction, correction, and instruction. Although the 66 books had human writers with individual personalities and linguistic particularities, God authored those books by inspiring them to write His Word without error.

5
Bible and Reference Books

The Bible was originally written in Greek and Hebrew but it has been translated into many different English-language versions. You want to make certain that you have a solid, accurate translation. I recommend the *New American Standard Bible,* the *New King James Bible,* and the *New International Version.*

I also highly recommend the *Discovery Bible* (Moody Press), a New Testament *(New American Standard Bible)* which is an excellent help in getting closer to the original Greek (without having to learn the language). The volume points out major synonyms (revealing the full meaning of each word used contrasted with others that are not). It shows what kind of action there is in the verbs and which words were given emphasis by the original writers. Most of this is done right in the text so you can instantly find great gems.

Your study Bible should have cross-references (Scripture references in the margin which direct you to other, similar passages). It's also a good idea to obtain a Bible with good maps.

Probably the most important volume you should own, next to your Bible, is an exhaustive concordance. A concordance lists every word in the Bible by its reference address so that you can find any verse simply by looking up a key word. All the major translations have a concordance; so make certain you purchase one that is based upon the translation you are using.

A good one-volume Bible dictionary (or encyclopedia) is also an excellent help in your studies. Of course, there are an unlimited number of other study books on the market to improve your study.

6
How to Use This Book

General Instructions

It has been proven that we remember more when we write things down. Each method in this notebook requires you to record what you find. Even if you never look at these studies again, the act of writing them down will aid your memory in retaining these spiritual discoveries.

Don't expect answers to every question in each method. Although the questions are general, they will not all apply to every passage. When a question does not have an answer, write "NA" (not applicable) and continue.

Try to answer all the questions without the aid of other books or commentaries. It is more exciting to discover nuggets of truth for yourself than to have them handed to you on a platter. Use a Bible dictionary or handbook *only after* you have exhausted the information you can find in the Scriptures.

Always ask yourself why God caused each passage to be written. Although He deals with men differently in each age, His basic nature and message hasn't changed. Try to look beyond the obvious to find the basic, unchangeable principles which run throughout Scripture.

The Daily Log

The daily log will help you check your Bible study faithfulness. Each day as you begin your study, put the name of the method you are using opposite the current day of the month. In this way you can keep your approach to God's Word varied and interesting.

5-MINUTE METHODS

1. *Verse Glance*—Select and examine a single Bible verse.
2. *Proverbs Glance*—Choose a proverb and examine it for practical information.

3. *Meditation*—Select a passage upon which you will meditate throughout the day.
4. *Psalm Glance*—Pick a Psalm, skimming its contents, and then answer the quick questions about it.
5. *Paragraph Glance*—Take a Bible chapter and summarize in your own words what each paragraph is saying. Write the paragraph verse numbers on the left and your summary on the right.
6. *Prophecy Glance*—Select a prophecy book and write the paragraph verse numbers on the left and your summaries on the right. Put a circled "P" opposite each paragraph that actually predicts something.
7. *Paraphrase*—Pick a short passage and rewrite it in your own words. Try to read the Scripture in two different translations (neither of which should be a Bible paraphrase).

15-MINUTE METHODS
8. *Law Study*—Select an Old Testament law passage and examine the purpose and meaning of the original Jewish regulations in the light of the New Testament Scriptures (which you can find through cross-references).
9. *Prophecy Study*—Choose a passage that foretells some event (you might want to examine a passage you've discovered in your *Prophecy Glance* studies). Always look to see if there is more than one fulfillment for the prophecy.
10. *Epistle Study*—Select a short passage from a New Testament letter and dig into it, seeking to understand and apply its meaning.
11. *The Five W's*—You will look at a historical passage with the eye of a reporter trying to find out who, when, where, what, and why the event took place.
12. *Teachings of Jesus*—Select a passage in the gospels which contains a message or parable from Jesus, and look for the basic underlying teaching to apply to your life.
13. *Doctrine Study*—Select a doctrinal subject and using a concordance (look in the back of your Bible if you don't own a separate single-volume concordance) and cross-references find out everything you can on this subject.

14. *Book Study*—Select a Bible book and seek to understand the basic content, background and purpose of the book by skimming it all the way through. Once you have discovered all the information you can, you might want to use other books to supply the missing data.

Which Method to Use

Chapter seven will provide a list of suggested Bible passages for you to study with each method in this book. But if you have a passage you would like to study and don't know which method to use on it, you can select an appropriate method using this short guide:

For Law Books:
Law Study (15)
Paragraph Glance (5)
The Five W's (15)
Doctrine Study (15)

For Historical Books:
The Five W's (15)
Paragraph Glance (5)

For Poetry Books:
Psalm Glance (5)
Proverbs Glance (5)
Paraphrase (5)

For Prophetic Books:
Prophecy Glance (5)
Prophecy Study (15)

For Gospels:
Teachings of Jesus (15)
The Five W's (15)
Paraphrase Glance (5)
Doctrine Study (15)

For Epistles:
Epistle Study (15)
Meditation (5)
Verse Glance (5)
Paragraph Glance (5)
Paraphrase (5)
Doctrine Study (15)

For Devotional Studies:
Verse Glance (5)
Proverbs Glance (5)
Meditation (5)
Psalm Glance (5)
Paraphrase (5)

7
What to Study

This chapter contains some suggested study passages selected carefully to introduce you to the different parts of God's Word. Check off each passage as you study it. If you are not familiar with the contents of the Bible, you might want to begin with survey methods like *Paragraph* and *Prophecy Glance.*

1) **Verse Glance**
   - ☐ Ephesians 4:31
   - ☐ John 5:24
   - ☐ Jeremiah 33:3
   - ☐ Luke 12:22,23
   - ☐ Ephesians 2:10
   - ☐ Jeremiah 17:9,10
   - ☐ Philippians 2:3,4
   - ☐ Romans 1:18,19
   - ☐ 1 Corinthians 6:20
   - ☐ 1 John 3:14

   - ☐ Galatians 5:16,17
   - ☐ Ephesians 4:28
   - ☐ Romans 8:28,29
   - ☐ Galatians 6:3
   - ☐ Ecclesiastes 5:8
   - ☐ Isaiah 5:20,21
   - ☐ 2 Corinthians 10:5
   - ☐ 2 Corinthians 4:16
   - ☐ Acts 4:12
   - ☐ 2 Corinthians 13:5

2) **Proverbs Glance**
   - ☐ Proverbs 21:13
   - ☐ Proverbs 26:24-26
   - ☐ Proverbs 19:15
   - ☐ Proverbs 19:2
   - ☐ Proverbs 1:24-30
   - ☐ Proverbs 22:29
   - ☐ Proverbs 14:6
   - ☐ Proverbs 24:21
   - ☐ Proverbs 23:12
   - ☐ Proverbs 19:26

   - ☐ Proverbs 22:17-21
   - ☐ Proverbs 28:24
   - ☐ Proverbs 15:10
   - ☐ Proverbs 15:8
   - ☐ Proverbs 18:2
   - ☐ Proverbs 11:2
   - ☐ Proverbs 14:29
   - ☐ Proverbs 15:22
   - ☐ Proverbs 17:27
   - ☐ Proverbs 19:13

3) **Meditation**
   - ☐ James 2:14-26
   - ☐ Proverbs 7:6-23
   - ☐ Numbers 14:1-25

   - ☐ Galatians 5:16-26
   - ☐ John 1:1-18
   - ☐ Revelation 21:1-27

- [ ] Luke 11:1-13
- [ ] 2 Peter 1:1-11
- [ ] Mark 12:1-12
- [ ] Luke 11:42-54
- [ ] Revelation 1:1-8
- [ ] 2 Samuel 18:1-18
- [ ] 2 Samuel 18:19-33
- [ ] Acts 21:1-6
- [ ] Acts 21:17-36
- [ ] Acts 21:37-22:29
- [ ] Luke 3:1-20
- [ ] Matthew 22:1-14

- [ ] Job 26:1-14
- [ ] Job 40:1-24
- [ ] 2 Chronicles 1:1-17
- [ ] 1 Kings 17:1-24
- [ ] Luke 13:10-17
- [ ] Judges 6:7-32
- [ ] Judges 6:33-7:25
- [ ] Judges 8:1-35
- [ ] Judges 13:1-25
- [ ] Judges 14:1-20
- [ ] Judges 15:1-20
- [ ] Judges 16:1-31

4) Psalm Glance

- [ ] Psalm 104
- [ ] Psalm 51
- [ ] Psalm 119:1-8
- [ ] Psalm 119:97-104
- [ ] Psalm 119:105-112
- [ ] Psalm 124
- [ ] Psalm 98
- [ ] Psalm 84
- [ ] Psalm 128
- [ ] Psalm 95

- [ ] Psalm 11
- [ ] Psalm 100
- [ ] Psalm 104
- [ ] Psalm 6
- [ ] Psalm 144
- [ ] Psalm 73
- [ ] Psalm 9
- [ ] Psalm 62
- [ ] Psalm 119:9-16
- [ ] Psalm 148

5) Paragraph Glance

- [ ] Galatians 1
- [ ] Galatians 2
- [ ] Galatians 3
- [ ] Galatians 4
- [ ] Galatians 5
- [ ] Galatians 6
- [ ] Mark 1
- [ ] Mark 2
- [ ] Mark 3
- [ ] Mark 4
- [ ] Mark 5
- [ ] Mark 6
- [ ] Mark 7
- [ ] Mark 8
- [ ] Mark 9

- [ ] Mark 10
- [ ] Mark 11
- [ ] Mark 12
- [ ] Mark 13
- [ ] Mark 14
- [ ] 1 Samuel 1
- [ ] 1 Samuel 2
- [ ] 1 Samuel 3
- [ ] 1 Samuel 4
- [ ] 1 Samuel 5
- [ ] 1 Samuel 6
- [ ] 1 Samuel 7
- [ ] 1 Samuel 8
- [ ] 1 Samuel 9
- [ ] 1 Samuel 10

6) Prophecy Glance

- ☐ Daniel 7
- ☐ Daniel 8
- ☐ Daniel 9
- ☐ Daniel 10
- ☐ Daniel 11
- ☐ Daniel 12
- ☐ Joel 1
- ☐ Joel 2
- ☐ Joel 3
- ☐ Isaiah 1
- ☐ Isaiah 2
- ☐ Isaiah 3
- ☐ Isaiah 4
- ☐ Isaiah 5
- ☐ Isaiah 6
- ☐ Isaiah 7
- ☐ Isaiah 8
- ☐ Isaiah 9
- ☐ Isaiah 10
- ☐ Isaiah 11
- ☐ Isaiah 12
- ☐ Jeremiah 1
- ☐ Jeremiah 2
- ☐ Jeremiah 3
- ☐ Jeremiah 4
- ☐ Jeremiah 5
- ☐ Jeremiah 6
- ☐ Jeremiah 7
- ☐ Jeremiah 8
- ☐ Jeremiah 9

7) Paraphrase

- ☐ Romans 3:24,25
- ☐ 1 John 3:17,18
- ☐ 2 Peter 1:10,11
- ☐ Hebrews 12:11
- ☐ 1 Peter 2:20,21
- ☐ Romans 8:2,3
- ☐ 1 Timothy 1:15,16
- ☐ Ephesians 1:7-9
- ☐ Galatians 6:7-9
- ☐ Colossians 2:8-10
- ☐ 1 Timothy 6:6-9
- ☐ Philippians 2:14,15
- ☐ James 3:16-18
- ☐ Hebrews 12:14,15
- ☐ 1 Peter 3:8,9
- ☐ James 5:7-9
- ☐ Titus 1:15,16
- ☐ 2 Corinthians 9:6,7
- ☐ 1 Corinthians 13:4-7
- ☐ Romans 6:16-18

8) Law Study

- ☐ Leviticus 17:10-16
- ☐ Exodus 22:28-31
- ☐ Deuteronomy 14:22-27
- ☐ Leviticus 16:29-34
- ☐ Exodus 21:1-6
- ☐ Exodus 20:8-12
- ☐ Exodus 20:13-17
- ☐ Deuternomy 20:19,20
- ☐ Deuternomy 22:1-4
- ☐ Deuternomy 11:8-12

9) Prophecy Study

- ☐ Isaiah 49:1-7
- ☐ Matthew 24:15-27
- ☐ Isaiah 11:1-9
- ☐ 1 Thessalonians 4:13-18
- ☐ Revelation 13:11-18
- ☐ Daniel 9:24-27
- ☐ Daniel 11:40-45
- ☐ Revelation 11:1-13
- ☐ 2 Thessalonians 2:1-12
- ☐ Zechariah 3:6-10

10) Epistle Study

- [ ] 2 John 1-13
- [ ] 1 Peter 5:1-5
- [ ] 1 Peter 5:6-11
- [ ] Hebrews 12:1-13
- [ ] Philippians 4:10-19
- [ ] Ephesians 6:1-4
- [ ] 2 Corinthians 8:16-23
- [ ] 1 Corinthians 3:10-15
- [ ] Romans 12:3-8
- [ ] Romans 14:1-12

11) The Five W's

- [ ] Acts 17:16-34
- [ ] Mark 12:41-44
- [ ] John 20:1-10
- [ ] Acts 12:1-17
- [ ] 1 Kings 17:1-7
- [ ] Esther 1:10-22
- [ ] Acts 4:1-22
- [ ] Acts 21:7-14
- [ ] Exodus 1:8-14
- [ ] Joshua 10:6-11

12) Teachings of Jesus

- [ ] Matthew 13:47-50
- [ ] Luke 9:23-27
- [ ] Mark 4:21-25
- [ ] Matthew 18:21-35
- [ ] John 6:41-51
- [ ] John 12:44-50
- [ ] Mark 12:28-34
- [ ] Matthew 5:38-42
- [ ] Luke 20:9-18
- [ ] Luke 12:35-40

13) Topical Study

- [ ] Sin (Romans 3:10-18,23; 6:23; 1 Corinthians 15:56; 1 John 1:7-10)
- [ ] Repentance (Matthew 3:7-11; Luke 13:1-5; Revelation 3:19-20; Hebrews 12:17; 2 Corinthians 7:9-11; Acts 26:20)
- [ ] Temptation (2 Peter 2:9; 1 Corinthians 10:13; James 1:13-15; Matthew 4:1-10)
- [ ] Grace (Ephesians 2:1-10; Romans 6:14-15; Romans 11:6; 1 Corinthians 15:10; James 4:6; Jude 4)
- [ ] Spiritual Gifts (Romans 12:6-8; 1 Corinthians 12:8-10, 28-30; Ephesians 4:11; 1 Peter 4:9-11)
- [ ] Trinity (1 John 5:6-9; Matthew 3:16,17; 28:19; John 14:16-17; Genesis 1:26)
- [ ] Inspiration (2 Timothy 3:16; 2 Peter 2:20-21; 2 Samuel 23:2; Jeremiah 1:9; John 10:35)
- [ ] Deity of Jesus (John 1:1,18; 8:56-59; 20:28; 10:30; Romans 9:5; Hebrews 1:8)
- [ ] Divorce (1 Corinthians 7:10-15; Matthew 19:3-10; Malachi 2:13-15; Deuteronomy 24:1-4)

☐ Anxiety (Philippians 4:6; 1 Peter 5:6-7; Romans 8:28; Psalm 37:1-5)

14) Book Study
- ☐ John
- ☐ Jude
- ☐ Joshua
- ☐ Zechariah
- ☐ 1 Peter

What to Do Each Day

Each day as you study you will want to do three things:

- Select a passage and method from chapter eight.
- Record the method you are using in the Daily Log.
- Study the passage you have selected

Daily Log

"…they received the word with great eagerness, examining the Scriptures daily, to see whether these things were so."
Acts 17:11b NASV

Each day you study God's Word, list the name of the method used opposite the correct day. In this way you can tell how faithful you have been.

Month _____ Year _____

1 _____	22 _____	11 _____
2 _____	23 _____	12 _____
3 _____	24 _____	13 _____
4 _____	25 _____	14 _____
5 _____	26 _____	15 _____
6 _____	27 _____	16 _____
7 _____	28 _____	17 _____
8 _____	29 _____	18 _____
9 _____	30 _____	19 _____
10 _____	31 _____	20 _____
11 _____	Month _____	21 _____
12 _____	1 _____	22 _____
13 _____	2 _____	23 _____
14 _____	3 _____	24 _____
15 _____	4 _____	25 _____
16 _____	5 _____	26 _____
17 _____	6 _____	27 _____
18 _____	7 _____	28 _____
19 _____	8 _____	29 _____
20 _____	9 _____	30 _____
21 _____	10 _____	31 _____

Daily Log

"...they received the word with great eagerness, examining the Scriptures daily, to see whether these things were so."
Acts 17:11b NASV

Each day you study God's Word, list the name of the method used opposite the correct day. In this way you can tell how faithful you have been.

Month _____ Year_____

1_____	22 _____	11_____
2_____	23 _____	12_____
3_____	24 _____	13_____
4_____	25 _____	14_____
5_____	26 _____	15_____
6_____	27 _____	16_____
7_____	28 _____	17_____
8_____	29 _____	18_____
9_____	30 _____	19_____
10 _____	31 _____	20_____
11_____	Month _____	21_____
12_____	1 _____	22_____
13_____	2 _____	23_____
14_____	3 _____	24_____
15_____	4 _____	25_____
16_____	5 _____	26_____
17_____	6 _____	27_____
18_____	7 _____	28_____
19_____	8 _____	29_____
20_____	9 _____	30_____
21 _____	10 _____	31_____

Daily Log

"…they received the word with great eagerness, examining the Scriptures daily, to see whether these things were so."
Acts 17:11b NASV

Each day you study God's Word, list the name of the method used opposite the correct day. In this way you can tell how faithful you have been.

Month _____ Year _____

1 _____	22 _____	11 _____
2 _____	23 _____	12 _____
3 _____	24 _____	13 _____
4 _____	25 _____	14 _____
5 _____	26 _____	15 _____
6 _____	27 _____	16 _____
7 _____	28 _____	17 _____
8 _____	29 _____	18 _____
9 _____	30 _____	19 _____
10 _____	31 _____	20 _____
11 _____	Month _____	21 _____
12 _____	1 _____	22 _____
13 _____	2 _____	23 _____
14 _____	3 _____	24 _____
15 _____	4 _____	25 _____
16 _____	5 _____	26 _____
17 _____	6 _____	27 _____
18 _____	7 _____	28 _____
19 _____	8 _____	29 _____
20 _____	9 _____	30 _____
21 _____	10 _____	31 _____

Daily Log

"...they received the word with great eagerness, examining the Scriptures daily, to see whether these things were so."
Acts 17:11b NASV

Each day you study God's Word, list the name of the method used opposite the correct day. In this way you can tell how faithful you have been.

Month _____ Year_____

1 _____	22 _____	11_____
2 _____	23 _____	12_____
3 _____	24 _____	13_____
4 _____	25 _____	14_____
5 _____	26 _____	15_____
6 _____	27 _____	16_____
7 _____	28 _____	17_____
8 _____	29 _____	18_____
9 _____	30 _____	19_____
10 _____	31 _____	20_____
11_____	Month _____	21_____
12_____	1 _____	22_____
13_____	2 _____	23_____
14_____	3 _____	24_____
15_____	4 _____	25_____
16_____	5 _____	26_____
17_____	6 _____	27_____
18_____	7 _____	28_____
19_____	8 _____	29_____
20_____	9 _____	30_____
21 _____	10 _____	31_____

Daily Log

"...they received the word with great eagerness, examining the Scriptures daily, to see whether these things were so."
Acts 17:11b NASV

Each day you study God's Word, list the name of the method used opposite the correct day. In this way you can tell how faithful you have been.

Month _____ Year_____

1_____	22 _____	11_____
2_____	23 _____	12_____
3_____	24 _____	13_____
4_____	25 _____	14_____
5_____	26 _____	15_____
6_____	27 _____	16_____
7_____	28 _____	17_____
8_____	29 _____	18_____
9_____	30 _____	19_____
10 _____	31 _____	20_____
11_____	Month _____	21_____
12_____	1 _____	22_____
13_____	2 _____	23_____
14_____	3 _____	24_____
15_____	4 _____	25_____
16_____	5 _____	26_____
17_____	6 _____	27_____
18_____	7 _____	28_____
19_____	8 _____	29_____
20_____	9 _____	30_____
21 _____	10 _____	31_____

Daily Log

"...they received the word with great eagerness, examining the Scriptures daily, to see whether these things were so."
Acts 17:11b NASV

Each day you study God's Word, list the name of the method used opposite the correct day. In this way you can tell how faithful you have been.

Month _____ Year_____

1_____	22 _____	11_____
2_____	23 _____	12_____
3_____	24 _____	13_____
4_____	25 _____	14_____
5_____	26 _____	15_____
6_____	27 _____	16_____
7_____	28 _____	17_____
8_____	29 _____	18_____
9_____	30 _____	19_____
10 _____	31 _____	20_____
11_____	Month _____	21_____
12_____	1 _____	22_____
13_____	2 _____	23_____
14_____	3 _____	24_____
15_____	4 _____	25_____
16_____	5 _____	26_____
17_____	6 _____	27_____
18_____	7 _____	28_____
19_____	8 _____	29_____
20_____	9 _____	30_____
21 _____	10 _____	31_____

Verse Glance

Verse Selected _____ _Date_ _____

1. List any action verbs found in this verse. _____

_____

2. What or who is doing the action? _____

_____

3. What is the central message of this verse? _____

_____

_____

4. Are any promises or blessings given? _____

_____

_____

5. Do I reflect the message of this verse? _____

_____

_____

Verse Selected _____ _Date_ _____

1. List any action verbs found in this verse. _____

_____

2. What or who is doing the action? _____

_____

3. What is the central message of this verse? _____

_____

_____

4. Are any promises or blessings given? _____

_____

_____

5. Do I reflect the message of this verse? _____

_____

_____

Verse Glance

Verse Selected _____ _Date_ _____

_1._ List any action verbs found in this verse. _____
_____

_2._ What or who is doing the action? _____

_3._ What is the central message of this verse? _____
_____
_____

_4._ Are any promises or blessings given? _____
_____
_____

_5._ Do I reflect the message of this verse? _____
_____
_____

Verse Selected _____ _Date_ _____

_1._ List any action verbs found in this verse. _____
_____

_2._ What or who is doing the action? _____

_3._ What is the central message of this verse? _____
_____

_4._ Are any promises or blessings given? _____
_____

_5._ Do I reflect the message of this verse? _____
_____
_____

Verse Glance

Verse Selected _____ _Date_ _____

1. List any action verbs found in this verse. _____

2. What or who is doing the action? _____

3. What is the central message of this verse? _____
_____
_____

4. Are any promises or blessings given? _____
_____
_____

5. Do I reflect the message of this verse? _____
_____
_____

Verse Selected _____ _Date_ _____

1. List any action verbs found in this verse. _____

2. What or who is doing the action? _____

3. What is the central message of this verse? _____
_____
_____

4. Are any promises or blessings given? _____
_____
_____

5. Do I reflect the message of this verse? _____
_____
_____

Verse Glance

Verse Selected _____ _Date_ _____

1. List any action verbs found in this verse. _____

2. What or who is doing the action? _____

3. What is the central message of this verse? _____

_____

4. Are any promises or blessings given? _____

_____

5. Do I reflect the message of this verse? _____

_____

_____

Verse Selected _____ _Date_ _____

1. List any action verbs found in this verse. _____

2. What or who is doing the action? _____

3. What is the central message of this verse? _____

_____

4. Are any promises or blessings given? _____

_____

5. Do I reflect the message of this verse? _____

_____

_____

Verse Glance

Verse Selected _____ _Date_ _____

1. List any action verbs found in this verse. _____
_____

2. What or who is doing the action? _____
_____

3. What is the central message of this verse? _____
_____
_____

4. Are any promises or blessings given? _____
_____
_____

5. Do I reflect the message of this verse? _____
_____
_____

Verse Selected _____ _Date_ _____

1. List any action verbs found in this verse. _____
_____

2. What or who is doing the action? _____
_____

3. What is the central message of this verse? _____
_____
_____

4. Are any promises or blessings given? _____
_____
_____

5. Do I reflect the message of this verse? _____
_____
_____

Verse Glance

Verse Selected _____ _Date_ _____

1. List any action verbs found in this verse. _____

2. What or who is doing the action? _____

3. What is the central message of this verse? _____

4. Are any promises or blessings given? _____

5. Do I reflect the message of this verse? _____

Verse Selected _____ _Date_ _____

1. List any action verbs found in this verse. _____

2. What or who is doing the action? _____

3. What is the central message of this verse? _____

4. Are any promises or blessings given? _____

5. Do I reflect the message of this verse? _____

Verse Selected _____ _Date_ _____

1. List any action verbs found in this verse. _____

_____

2. What or who is doing the action? _____

_____

3. What is the central message of this verse? _____

_____

_____

4. Are any promises or blessings given? _____

_____

_____

5. Do I reflect the message of this verse? _____

_____

_____

Verse Selected _____ _Date_ _____

1. List any action verbs found in this verse. _____

_____

2. What or who is doing the action? _____

_____

3. What is the central message of this verse? _____

_____

_____

4. Are any promises or blessings given? _____

_____

_____

5. Do I reflect the message of this verse? _____

_____

_____

Verse Glance

Verse Selected _____ _Date_ _____

1. List any action verbs found in this verse. _____

_____

2. What or who is doing the action? _____

_____

3. What is the central message of this verse? _____

_____

_____

4. Are any promises or blessings given? _____

_____

_____

5. Do I reflect the message of this verse? _____

_____

_____

Verse Selected _____ _Date_ _____

1. List any action verbs found in this verse. _____

_____

2. What or who is doing the action? _____

_____

3. What is the central message of this verse? _____

_____

_____

4. Are any promises or blessings given? _____

_____

_____

5. Do I reflect the message of this verse? _____

_____

_____

Verse Glance

Verse Selected _____ _Date_ _____

1. List any action verbs found in this verse. _____

_____

2. What or who is doing the action? _____

_____

3. What is the central message of this verse? _____

_____

_____

4. Are any promises or blessings given? _____

_____

_____

5. Do I reflect the message of this verse? _____

_____

_____

Verse Selected _____ _Date_ _____

1. List any action verbs found in this verse. _____

_____

2. What or who is doing the action? _____

3. What is the central message of this verse? _____

_____

_____

4. Are any promises or blessings given? _____

_____

5. Do I reflect the message of this verse? _____

_____

_____

Verse Glance

Verse Selected _____ _Date_ _____
1. List any action verbs found in this verse. _____
_____

2. What or who is doing the action? _____
_____

3. What is the central message of this verse? _____
_____
_____

4. Are any promises or blessings given? _____
_____
_____

5. Do I reflect the message of this verse? _____
_____
_____

Verse Selected _____ _Date_ _____
1. List any action verbs found in this verse. _____
_____

2. What or who is doing the action? _____
_____

3. What is the central message of this verse? _____
_____
_____

4. Are any promises or blessings given? _____
_____
_____

5. Do I reflect the message of this verse? _____
_____
_____

Proverbs Glance 5 minutes

Proverb Selected _____ _Date_ _____

1. What positive qualities are displayed? _____

_____

2. What negative qualities are displayed? _____

_____

3. What basic principle is God teaching in this passage? _____

_____

_____

4. What other Scripture supports this principle? _____

_____

5. How can I benefit from this principle? _____

_____

_____

_____

Proverb Selected _____ _Date_ _____

1. What positive qualities are displayed? _____

_____

2. What negative qualities are displayed? _____

_____

3. What basic principle is God teaching in this passage? _____

_____

_____

4. What other Scripture supports this principle? _____

_____

5. How can I benefit from this principle? _____

_____

_____

_____

Proverbs Glance

Proverb Selected _____ *Date* _____

1. What positive qualities are displayed? _____

2. What negative qualities are displayed? _____

3. What basic principle is God teaching in this passage? _____

4. What other Scripture supports this principle? _____

5. How can I benefit from this principle? _____

Proverb Selected _____ *Date* _____

1. What positive qualities are displayed? _____

2. What negative qualities are displayed? _____

3. What basic principle is God teaching in this passage? _____

4. What other Scripture supports this principle? _____

5. How can I benefit from this principle? _____

Proverbs Glance

Proverb Selected _____ *Date* _____

1. What positive qualities are displayed? _____

_____

2. What negative qualities are displayed? _____

_____

3. What basic principle is God teaching in this passage? _____

_____

_____

4. What other Scripture supports this principle? _____

_____

5. How can I benefit from this principle? _____

_____

_____

_____

Proverb Selected _____ *Date* _____

1. What positive qualities are displayed? _____

_____

2. What negative qualities are displayed? _____

_____

3. What basic principle is God teaching in this passage? _____

_____

_____

4. What other Scripture supports this principle? _____

_____

5. How can I benefit from this principle? _____

_____

_____

_____

Proverbs Glance   5 minutes

Proverb Selected _____ _Date_ _____

1. What positive qualities are displayed? _____

_____

2. What negative qualities are displayed? _____

_____

3. What basic principle is God teaching in this passage? _____

_____

_____

4. What other Scripture supports this principle? ____ _____

_____

5. How can I benefit from this principle? _____

_____

_____

_____

Proverb Selected _____ _Date_ _____

1. What positive qualities are displayed? _____

_____

2. What negative qualities are displayed? _____

_____

3. What basic principle is God teaching in this passage? _____

_____

_____

4. What other Scripture supports this principle? _____

_____

5. How can I benefit from this principle? _____

_____

_____

Proverbs Glance

Proverb Selected _____ _Date_ _____

1. What positive qualities are displayed? _____

_____

2. What negative qualities are displayed? _____

_____

3. What basic principle is God teaching in this passage? _____

_____

_____

4. What other Scripture supports this principle? _____

_____

5. How can I benefit from this principle? _____

_____

_____

_____

Proverb Selected _____ _Date_ _____

1. What positive qualities are displayed? _____

_____

2. What negative qualities are displayed? _____

_____

3. What basic principle is God teaching in this passage? _____

_____

_____

4. What other Scripture supports this principle? _____

_____

5. How can I benefit from this principle? _____

_____

_____

_____

Proverbs Glance

Proverb Selected _____ _Date_ _____

1. What positive qualities are displayed? _____

2. What negative qualities are displayed? _____

3. What basic principle is God teaching in this passage? _____

4. What other Scripture supports this principle? _____

5. How can I benefit from this principle? _____

Proverb Selected _____ _Date_ _____

1. What positive qualities are displayed? _____

2. What negative qualities are displayed? _____

3. What basic principle is God teaching in this passage? _____

4. What other Scripture supports this principle? _____

5. How can I benefit from this principle? _____

Proverbs Glance

Proverb Selected _____ _Date_ _____

1. What positive qualities are displayed?_____

_____

2. What negative qualities are displayed?_____

3. What basic principle is God teaching in this passage?_____

_____

_____

4. What other Scripture supports this principle?_____

_____

5. How can I benefit from this principle? _____

_____

_____

_____

Proverb Selected _____ _Date_ _____

1. What positive qualities are displayed?_____

2. What negative qualities are displayed? _____

_____

3. What basic principle is God teaching in this passage?_____

_____

_____

4. What other Scripture supports this principle?_____

_____

5. How can I benefit from this principle? _____

_____

_____

_____

Proverbs Glance   5 minutes

Proverb Selected _____ *Date* _____

1. What positive qualities are displayed? _____

_____

2. What negative qualities are displayed? _____

_____

3. What basic principle is God teaching in this passage? _____

_____

_____

4. What other Scripture supports this principle? _____

_____

5. How can I benefit from this principle? _____

_____

_____

_____

Proverb Selected _____ *Date* _____

1. What positive qualities are displayed? _____

_____

2. What negative qualities are displayed? _____

_____

3. What basic principle is God teaching in this passage? _____

_____

_____

4. What other Scripture supports this principle? _____

_____

5. How can I benefit from this principle? _____

_____

_____

_____

Proverbs Glance

Proverb Selected _____ _Date_ _____

1. What positive qualities are displayed? _____

2. What negative qualities are displayed? _____

3. What basic principle is God teaching in this passage? _____

4. What other Scripture supports this principle? _____

5. How can I benefit from this principle? _____

Proverb Selected _____ _Date_ _____

1. What positive qualities are displayed? _____

2. What negative qualities are displayed? _____

3. What basic principle is God teaching in this passage? _____

4. What other Scripture supports this principle? _____

5. How can I benefit from this principle? _____

Proverbs Glance

Proverb Selected _____ _Date_ _____

1. What positive qualities are displayed?_____

_____

2. What negative qualities are displayed?_____

_____

3. What basic principle is God teaching in this passage?_____

_____

_____

4. What other Scripture supports this principle?_____

_____

5. How can I benefit from this principle? _____

_____

_____

_____

Proverb Selected _____ _Date_ _____

1. What positive qualities are displayed?_____

_____

2. What negative qualities are displayed? _____

_____

3. What basic principle is God teaching in this passage?_____

_____

_____

4. What other Scripture supports this principle?_____

_____

5. How can I benefit from this principle?_____

_____

_____

_____

Meditation

Passage Selected_____ *Date*_____

1. Read the passage, considering the meaning of each phrase.

2. Which verse do I want to meditate on today?_____

_____

_____

3. What God gave me from this passage:_____

_____

_____

_____

Passage Selected_____ *Date*_____

1. Read the passage, considering the meaning of each phrase.

2. Which verse do I want to meditate on today?_____

_____

_____

3. What God gave me from this passage:_____

_____

_____

_____

Passage Selected_____ *Date*_____

1. Read the passage, considering the meaning of each phrase.

2. Which verse do I want to meditate on today?_____

_____

_____

3. What God gave me from this passage: _____

_____

_____

_____

Meditation

Passage Selected_____ _Date_____

1. Read the passage, considering the meaning of each phrase.
2. Which verse do I want to meditate on today?_____
_____
_____

3. What God gave me from this passage:_____
_____
_____
_____

Passage Selected_____ _Date_____

1. Read the passage, considering the meaning of each phrase.
2. Which verse do I want to meditate on today?_____
_____
_____

3. What God gave me from this passage:_____
_____
_____
_____

Passage Selected_____ _Date_____

1. Read the passage, considering the meaning of each phrase.
2. Which verse do I want to meditate on today?_____
_____
_____

3. What God gave me from this passage:_____
_____
_____
_____

Meditation

Passage Selected_____ _Date_____

1. Read the passage, considering the meaning of each phrase.

2. Which verse do I want to meditate on today?_____
_____
_____

3. What God gave me from this passage:_____
_____
_____
_____

Passage Selected_____ _Date_____

1. Read the passage, considering the meaning of each phrase.

2. Which verse do I want to meditate on today?_____
_____
_____

3. What God gave me from this passage:_____
_____
_____
_____

Passage Selected_____ _Date_____

1. Read the passage, considering the meaning of each phrase.

2. Which verse do I want to meditate on today?_____
_____
_____

3. What God gave me from this passage:_____
_____
_____
_____

Meditation

Passage Selected_____ *Date*_____

1. Read the passage, considering the meaning of each phrase.

2. Which verse do I want to meditate on today?_____
_____
_____

3. What God gave me from this passage:_____
_____
_____
_____

Passage Selected_____ *Date*_____

1. Read the passage, considering the meaning of each phrase.

2. Which verse do I want to meditate on today?_____
_____
_____

3. What God gave me from this passage: _____
_____
_____
_____

Passage Selected_____ *Date*_____

1. Read the passage, considering the meaning of each phrase.

2. Which verse do I want to meditate on today?_____
_____
_____

3. What God gave me from this passage: _____
_____
_____
_____

Meditation

Passage Selected _____ _Date_ _____

1. Read the passage, considering the meaning of each phrase.
2. Which verse do I want to meditate on today? _____

_____

_____

3. What God gave me from this passage: _____

_____

_____

_____

Passage Selected _____ _Date_ _____

1. Read the passage, considering the meaning of each phrase.
2. Which verse do I want to meditate on today? _____

_____

_____

3. What God gave me from this passage: _____

_____

_____

_____

Passage Selected _____ _Date_ _____

1. Read the passage, considering the meaning of each phrase.
2. Which verse do I want to meditate on today? _____

_____

_____

3. What God gave me from this passage: _____

_____

_____

_____

Meditation

Passage Selected _____ _Date_ _____

1. Read the passage, considering the meaning of each phrase.
2. Which verse do I want to meditate on today? _____

_____

3. What God gave me from this passage: _____

_____

_____

_____

Passage Selected _____ _Date_ _____

1. Read the passage, considering the meaning of each phrase.
2. Which verse do I want to meditate on today? _____

_____

_____

3. What God gave me from this passage: _____

_____

_____

_____

Passage Selected _____ _Date_ _____

1. Read the passage, considering the meaning of each phrase.
2. Which verse do I want to meditate on today? _____

_____

3. What God gave me from this passage: _____

_____

_____

_____

Meditation

Passage Selected_____ *Date*_____

1. Read the passage, considering the meaning of each phrase.

2. Which verse do I want to meditate on today?_____
_____
_____

3. What God gave me from this passage:_____
_____
_____
_____

Passage Selected_____ *Date*_____

1. Read the passage, considering the meaning of each phrase.

2. Which verse do I want to meditate on today?_____
_____
_____

3. What God gave me from this passage:_____
_____
_____
_____

Passage Selected_____ *Date*_____

1. Read the passage, considering the meaning of each phrase.

2. Which verse do I want to meditate on today?_____
_____
_____

3. What God gave me from this passage:_____
_____
_____
_____

Meditation

Passage Selected_____ _Date_____

1. Read the passage, considering the meaning of each phrase.
2. Which verse do I want to meditate on today?_____

_____

_____

3. What God gave me from this passage:_____

_____

_____

_____

Passage Selected_____ _Date_____

1. Read the passage, considering the meaning of each phrase.
2. Which verse do I want to meditate on today?_____

_____

_____

3. What God gave me from this passage:_____

_____

_____

_____

Passage Selected_____ _Date_____

1. Read the passage, considering the meaning of each phrase.
2. Which verse do I want to meditate on today?_____

_____

_____

3. What God gave me from this passage:_____

_____

_____

_____

Meditation

Passage Selected_____ *Date*_____

1. Read the passage, considering the meaning of each phrase.
2. Which verse do I want to meditate on today?_____
_____

_____

3. What God gave me from this passage:_____
_____

_____

_____

Passage Selected_____ *Date*_____

1. Read the passage, considering the meaning of each phrase.
2. Which verse do I want to meditate on today?_____
_____

_____

3. What God gave me from this passage:_____
_____

_____

_____

Passage Selected_____ *Date*_____

1. Read the passage, considering the meaning of each phrase.
2. Which verse do I want to meditate on today?_____
_____

_____

3. What God gave me from this passage:_____
_____

_____

_____

Meditation

Passage Selected_____ Date_____

1. Read the passage, considering the meaning of each phrase.

2. Which verse do I want to meditate on today?_____

_____

3. What God gave me from this passage:_____

_____

_____

_____

Passage Selected_____ Date_____

1. Read the passage, considering the meaning of each phrase.

2. Which verse do I want to meditate on today?_____

_____

3. What God gave me from this passage:_____

_____

_____

_____

Passage Selected_____ Date_____

1. Read the passage, considering the meaning of each phrase.

2. Which verse do I want to meditate on today?_____

_____

3. What God gave me from this passage:_____

_____

_____

_____

Psalm Glance

Psalm Selected _____ _Date_ _____

1. Check the type of Psalm:
   - ☐ Messianic or Prophetic   ☐ Nature
   - ☐ Instructional   ☐ Praise
   - ☐ Historical   ☐ Prayer

2. What is this Psalm about? _____
_____
_____

3. Are any blessings promised? _____
_____
_____

4. What does this Psalm say to me? _____
_____
_____

Psalm Selected _____ _Date_ _____

1. Check the type of Psalm:
   - ☐ Messianic or Prophetic   ☐ Nature
   - ☐ Instructional   ☐ Praise
   - ☐ Historical   ☐ Prayer

2. What is this Psalm about? _____
_____
_____

3. Are any blessings promised? _____
_____
_____

4. What does this Psalm say to me? _____
_____
_____

Psalm Glance

Psalm Selected _____ _Date_ _____

1. Check the type of Psalm:
   - ☐ Messianic or Prophetic   ☐ Nature
   - ☐ Instructional   ☐ Praise
   - ☐ Historical   ☐ Prayer

2. What is this Psalm about? _____
_____
_____

3. Are any blessings promised? _____
_____
_____

4. What does this Psalm say to me? _____
_____
_____

Psalm Selected _____ _Date_ _____

1. Check the type of Psalm:
   - ☐ Messianic or Prophetic   ☐ Nature
   - ☐ Instructional   ☐ Praise
   - ☐ Historical   ☐ Prayer

2. What is this Psalm about? _____
_____
_____

3. Arc any blessings promised? _____
_____
_____

4. What does this Psalm say to me? _____
_____
_____

Psalm Glance

Psalm Selected _____ _Date_ _____

1. Check the type of Psalm:
   - ☐ Messianic or Prophetic   ☐ Nature
   - ☐ Instructional   ☐ Praise
   - ☐ Historical   ☐ Prayer
2. What is this Psalm about? _____
   _____
   _____
3. Are any blessings promised? _____
   _____
   _____
4. What does this Psalm say to me? _____
   _____
   _____

Psalm Selected _____ _Date_ _____

1. Check the type of Psalm:
   - ☐ Messianic or Prophetic   ☐ Nature
   - ☐ Instructional   ☐ Praise
   - ☐ Historical   ☐ Prayer
2. What is this Psalm about? _____
   _____
   _____
3. Are any blessings promised? _____
   _____
   _____
4. What does this Psalm say to me? _____
   _____
   _____

Psalm Glance

Psalm Selected _____ _Date_ _____

1. Check the type of Psalm:
   - ☐ Messianic or Prophetic   ☐ Nature
   - ☐ Instructional   ☐ Praise
   - ☐ Historical   ☐ Prayer

2. What is this Psalm about? _____
   _____
   _____

3. Are any blessings promised? _____
   _____
   _____

4. What does this Psalm say to me? _____
   _____
   _____

Psalm Selected _____ _Date_ _____

1. Check the type of Psalm:
   - ☐ Messianic or Prophetic   ☐ Nature
   - ☐ Instructional   ☐ Praise
   - ☐ Historical   ☐ Prayer

2. What is this Psalm about? _____
   _____
   _____

3. Are any blessings promised? _____
   _____
   _____

4. What does this Psalm say to me? _____
   _____
   _____

Psalm Glance

Psalm Selected _____ _Date_ _____

1. Check the type of Psalm:
   ☐ Messianic or Prophetic   ☐ Nature
   ☐ Instructional   ☐ Praise
   ☐ Historical   ☐ Prayer

2. What is this Psalm about? _____
   _____
   _____

3. Are any blessings promised? _____
   _____
   _____

4. What does this Psalm say to me? _____
   _____
   _____

Psalm Selected _____ _Date_ _____

1. Check the type of Psalm:
   ☐ Messianic or Prophetic   ☐ Nature
   ☐ Instructional   ☐ Praise
   ☐ Historical   ☐ Prayer

2. What is this Psalm about? _____
   _____
   _____

3. Are any blessings promised? _____
   _____
   _____

4. What does this Psalm say to me? _____
   _____
   _____

Psalm Glance

 5 minutes

Psalm Selected_____ _Date_____

1. Check the type of Psalm:

   ☐ Messianic or Prophetic   ☐ Nature

   ☐ Instructional   ☐ Praise

   ☐ Historical   ☐ Prayer

2. What is this Psalm about?_____

_____

_____

3. Are any blessings promised?_____

_____

_____

4. What does this Psalm say to me?_____

_____

_____

Psalm Selected _____ _____ _Date_____

1. Check the type of Psalm:

   ☐ Messianic or Prophetic   ☐ Nature

   ☐ Instructional   ☐ Praise

   ☐ Historical   ☐ Prayer

2. What is this Psalm about?_____

_____

_____

3. Are any blessings promised?_____

_____

_____

4. What does this Psalm say to me?_____

_____

_____

Psalm Glance

Psalm Selected _____ _Date_ _____

1. Check the type of Psalm:
   - ☐ Messianic or Prophetic   ☐ Nature
   - ☐ Instructional   ☐ Praise
   - ☐ Historical   ☐ Prayer

2. What is this Psalm about? _____
   _____
   _____

3. Are any blessings promised? _____
   _____
   _____

4. What does this Psalm say to me? _____
   _____
   _____

Psalm Selected _____ _Date_ _____

1. Check the type of Psalm:
   - ☐ Messianic or Prophetic   ☐ Nature
   - ☐ Instructional   ☐ Praise
   - ☐ Historical   ☐ Prayer

2. What is this Psalm about? _____
   _____
   _____

3. Are any blessings promised? _____
   _____
   _____

4. What does this Psalm say to me? _____
   _____
   _____

Psalm Glance

Psalm Selected_____ *Date*_____

1. Check the type of Psalm:
   - ☐ Messianic or Prophetic   ☐ Nature
   - ☐ Instructional   ☐ Praise
   - ☐ Historical   ☐ Prayer

2. What is this Psalm about?_____

_____

_____

3. Are any blessings promised?_____

_____

_____

4. What does this Psalm say to me?_____

_____

_____

Psalm Selected_____ *Date*_____

1. Check the type of Psalm:
   - ☐ Messianic or Prophetic   ☐ Nature
   - ☐ Instructional   ☐ Praise
   - ☐ Historical   ☐ Prayer

2. What is this Psalm about?_____

_____

_____

3. Are any blessings promised?_____

_____

_____

4. What does this Psalm say to me?_____

_____

_____

Psalm Glance

Psalm Selected _____ *Date* _____

1. Check the type of Psalm:
   - ☐ Messianic or Prophetic   ☐ Nature
   - ☐ Instructional   ☐ Praise
   - ☐ Historical   ☐ Prayer
2. What is this Psalm about? _____
   _____
   _____
3. Are any blessings promised? _____
   _____
   _____
4. What does this Psalm say to me? _____
   _____
   _____

Psalm Selected _____ *Date* _____

1. Check the type of Psalm:
   - ☐ Messianic or Prophetic   ☐ Nature
   - ☐ Instructional   ☐ Praise
   - ☐ Historical   ☐ Prayer
2. What is this Psalm about? _____
   _____
   _____
3. Are any blessings promised? _____
   _____
   _____
4. What does this Psalm say to me? _____
   _____
   _____

Psalm Glance

Psalm Selected _____ *Date* _____

1. Check the type of Psalm:
   - ☐ Messianic or Prophetic   ☐ Nature
   - ☐ Instructional   ☐ Praise
   - ☐ Historical   ☐ Prayer

2. What is this Psalm about? _____
_____
_____

3. Are any blessings promised? _____
_____
_____

4. What does this Psalm say to me? _____
_____
_____

Psalm Selected _____ *Date* _____

1. Check the type of Psalm:
   - ☐ Messianic or Prophetic   ☐ Nature
   - ☐ Instructional   ☐ Praise
   - ☐ Historical   ☐ Prayer

2. What is this Psalm about? _____
_____
_____

3. Are any blessings promised? _____
_____
_____

4. What does this Psalm say to me? _____
_____
_____

Paragraph Glance 5 minutes

Book _____ **Number of Chapters** _____

Write the paragraph references on the left. Summarize the contents of each paragraph on the right. Date each entry.

Reference	_Summary_	_Date_

Paragraph Glance 5 minutes

Book _____ **Number of Chapters** _____

Write the paragraph references on the left. Summarize the contents of each paragraph on the right. Date each entry.

Reference	*Summary*	*Date*

Paragraph Glance 5 minutes

Book   **Number of Chapters**

Write the paragraph references on the left. Summarize the contents of each paragraph on the right. Date each entry.

Reference   Summary   Date

Paragraph Glance *5 minutes*

Book **Number of Chapters**

Write the paragraph references on the left. Summarize the contents of each paragraph on the right. Date each entry.

Reference   Summary   Date

_____

_____

_____

_____

_____

_____

_____

_____

_____

_____

_____

_____

_____

_____

_____

_____

_____

_____

_____

_____

Paragraph Glance 5 minutes

Book   **Number of Chapters**

Write the paragraph references on the left. Summarize the contents of
each paragraph on the right. Date each entry.

Reference   Summary   Date

Paragraph Glance 5 minutes

Book   **Number of Chapters**

Write the paragraph references on the left. Summarize the contents of each paragraph on the right. Date each entry.

Reference   Summary   Date

Paragraph Glance *5 minutes*

Book   **Number of Chapters**

Write the paragraph references on the left. Summarize the contents of
each paragraph on the right. Date each entry.

Reference   Summary   Date

Paragraph Glance 5 minutes

Book **Number of Chapters**

Write the paragraph references on the left. Summarize the contents of each paragraph on the right. Date each entry.

Reference   Summary   Date

Paragraph Glance 5 minutes

Book   **Number of Chapters**

Write the paragraph references on the left. Summarize the contents of each paragraph on the right. Date each entry.

Reference   Summary   Date

Paragraph Glance 5 minutes

Book   **Number of Chapters**

Write the paragraph references on the left. Summarize the contents of each paragraph on the right. Date each entry.

Reference   Summary   Date

Book _____ **Number of Chapters** _____

Write the paragraph references on the left. Summarize the contents of each paragraph on the right. Date each entry.

Reference	*Summary*	*Date*

Paragraph Glance 5 minutes

Book _____ **Number of Chapters** _____

Write the paragraph references on the left. Summarize the contents of each paragraph on the right. Date each entry.

Reference   _Summary_   _Date_

Paragraph Glance 5 minutes

Book _____ **Number of Chapters** _____

Write the paragraph references on the left. Summarize the contents of each paragraph on the right. Date each entry.

Reference   _Summary_   _Date_

Paragraph Glance 5 minutes

Book _____ **Number of Chapters** _____

Write the paragraph references on the left. Summarize the contents of each paragraph on the right. Date each entry.

Reference   _Summary_   _Date_

Paragraph Glance 5 minutes

Book _____ **Number of Chapters** _____

Write the paragraph references on the left. Summarize the contents of each paragraph on the right. Date each entry.

Reference   _Summary_   _Date_

_____
_____
_____
_____
_____
_____
_____
_____
_____
_____
_____
_____
_____
_____
_____
_____
_____
_____
_____
_____
_____
_____
_____
_____

Paragraph Glance · 5 minutes

Book _____ **Number of Chapters** _____

Write the paragraph references on the left. Summarize the contents of each paragraph on the right. Date each entry.

Reference   _Summary_   _Date_

Paragraph Glance 5 minutes

Book _____ **Number of Chapters** _____

Write the paragraph references on the left. Summarize the contents of each paragraph on the right. Date each entry.

Reference   _Summary_   _Date_

Paragraph Glance 5 minutes

Book _____ **Number of Chapters** _____

Write the paragraph references on the left. Summarize the contents of each paragraph on the right. Date each entry.

Reference	*Summary*	*Date*

Paragraph Glance 5 minutes

Book _____ **Number of Chapters** _____

Write the paragraph references on the left. Summarize the contents of each paragraph on the right. Date each entry.

Reference   *Summary*   *Date*

_____

_____

_____

_____

_____

_____

_____

_____

_____

_____

_____

_____

_____

_____

_____

_____

_____

_____

_____

_____

_____

_____

Paragraph Glance 5 minutes

Book _____ **Number of Chapters** _____

Write the paragraph references on the left. Summarize the contents of each paragraph on the right. Date each entry.

Reference	Summary	Date

Prophecy Glance

Book Selected _____

1. Write the passage references on the left.
2. Summarize the contents of each paragraph. If it contains a prophecy write "P" at the right.
3. Spend no more than 5 minutes per passage.

Reference   *Summary*   *Date*

_____

_____

_____

_____

_____

_____

_____

_____

_____

_____

_____

_____

_____

_____

_____

_____

_____

_____

_____

Prophecy Glance

Book Selected _____

1. Write the passage references on the left.
2. Summarize the contents of each paragraph. If it contains a prophecy write "P" at the right.
3. Spend no more than 5 minutes per passage.

Reference	Summary	Date

Prophecy Glance

Book Selected _____

1. Write the passage references on the left.
2. Summarize the contents of each paragraph. If it contains a prophecy write "P" at the right.
3. Spend no more than 5 minutes per passage.

Reference	Summary	Date

Prophecy Glance 5 minutes

Book Selected _____

1. Write the passage references on the left.
2. Summarize the contents of each paragraph. If it contains a prophecy write "P" at the right.
3. Spend no more than 5 minutes per passage.

Reference	Summary	Date

Prophecy Glance

Book Selected _____

1. Write the passage references on the left.
2. Summarize the contents of each paragraph. If it contains a prophecy write "P" at the right.
3. Spend no more than 5 minutes per passage.

Reference	Summary	Date

Prophecy Glance

Book Selected _____

1. Write the passage references on the left.
2. Summarize the contents of each paragraph. If it contains a prophecy write "P" at the right.
3. Spend no more than 5 minutes per passage.

Reference	*Summary*	*Date*

Prophecy Glance

Book Selected _____

1. Write the passage references on the left.
2. Summarize the contents of each paragraph. If it contains a prophecy write "P" at the right.
3. Spend no more than 5 minutes per passage.

Reference	Summary	Date

Prophecy Glance

Book Selected _____

1. Write the passage references on the left.
2. Summarize the contents of each paragraph. If it contains a prophecy write "P" at the right.
3. Spend no more than 5 minutes per passage.

Reference	Summary	Date

Prophecy Glance 5 minutes

Book Selected _____

1. Write the passage references on the left.
2. Summarize the contents of each paragraph. If it contains a prophecy write "P" at the right.
3. Spend no more than 5 minutes per passage.

Reference	Summary	Date

Prophecy Glance

Book Selected _____

1. Write the passage references on the left.
2. Summarize the contents of each paragraph. If it contains a prophecy write "P" at the right.
3. Spend no more than 5 minutes per passage.

Reference	Summary	Date

Prophecy Glance

Book Selected _____

1. Write the passage references on the left.
2. Summarize the contents of each paragraph. If it contains a prophecy write "P" at the right.
3. Spend no more than 5 minutes per passage.

Reference	Summary	Date

Prophecy Glance

Book Selected _____

1. Write the passage references on the left.
2. Summarize the contents of each paragraph. If it contains a prophecy write "P" at the right.
3. Spend no more than 5 minutes per passage.

Reference	Summary	Date

Prophecy Glance   5 minutes

Book Selected _____

1. Write the passage references on the left.
2. Summarize the contents of each paragraph. If it contains a prophecy write "P" at the right.
3. Spend no more than 5 minutes per passage.

Reference   *Summary*   *Date*

_____

_____

_____

_____

_____

_____

_____

_____

_____

_____

_____

_____

_____

_____

_____

_____

_____

_____

_____

_____

_____

_____

_____

Prophecy Glance

Book Selected _____

1. Write the passage references on the left.
2. Summarize the contents of each paragraph. If it contains a prophecy write "P" at the right.
3. Spend no more than 5 minutes per passage.

Reference	Summary	Date

Prophecy Glance   5 minutes

Book Selected _____

1. Write the passage references on the left.
2. Summarize the contents of each paragraph. If it contains a prophecy write "P" at the right.
3. Spend no more than 5 minutes per passage.

Reference	Summary	Date

Prophecy Glance

Book Selected _____

1. Write the passage references on the left.
2. Summarize the contents of each paragraph. If it contains a prophecy write "P" at the right.
3. Spend no more than 5 minutes per passage.

Reference	Summary	Date

Prophecy Glance

5 minutes

Book Selected _____

1. Write the passage references on the left.
2. Summarize the contents of each paragraph. If it contains a prophecy write "P" at the right.
3. Spend no more than 5 minutes per passage.

Reference	Summary	Date

Prophecy Glance

Book Selected _____

1. Write the passage references on the left.
2. Summarize the contents of each paragraph. If it contains a prophecy write "P" at the right.
3. Spend no more than 5 minutes per passage.

Reference	Summary	Date

Prophecy Glance
5 minutes

Book Selected _____

1. Write the passage references on the left.
2. Summarize the contents of each paragraph. If it contains a prophecy write "P" at the right.
3. Spend no more than 5 minutes per passage.

Reference	Summary	Date

Prophecy Glance

Book Selected _____

1. Write the passage references on the left.
2. Summarize the contents of each paragraph. If it contains a prophecy write "P" at the right.
3. Spend no more than 5 minutes per passage.

Reference	Summary	Date

Paraphrase

Verses Selected _____ _Date_ _____

1. I am using the following two translations: _____

_____

2. Here is my paraphrase of the passage: _____

_____

_____

_____

_____

_____

_____

_____

_____

Verses Selected _____ _Date_ _____

1. I am using the following two translations: _____

_____

2. Here is my paraphrase of the passage: _____

_____

_____

_____

_____

_____

_____

_____

_____

Paraphrase

Verses Selected _____ _Date_ _____

1. I am using the following two translations: _____

_____

2. Here is my paraphrase of the passage: _____

_____

_____

_____

_____

_____

_____

_____

_____

_____

Verses Selected _____ _Date_ _____

1. I am using the following two translations: _____

_____

2. Here is my paraphrase of the passage: _____

_____

_____

_____

_____

_____

_____

_____

_____

_____

Paraphrase

Verses Selected _____ *Date* _____

1. I am using the following two translations: _____

_____

2. Here is my paraphrase of the passage: _____

_____

_____

_____

_____

_____

_____

_____

_____

_____

Verses Selected _____ *Date* _____

1. I am using the following two translations: _____

_____

2. Here is my paraphrase of the passage: _____

_____

_____

_____

_____

_____

_____

_____

_____

_____

Paraphrase

Verses Selected _____ _Date_ _____

1. I am using the following two translations: _____

_____

2. Here is my paraphrase of the passage:_____

_____

_____

_____

_____

_____

_____

_____

_____

_____

Verses Selected _____ _Date_ _____

1. I am using the following two translations:_____

_____

2. Here is my paraphrase of the passage:_____

_____

_____

_____

_____

_____

_____

_____

_____

Paraphrase

Verses Selected _____ _Date_____

1. I am using the following two translations: _____

_____

2. Here is my paraphrase of the passage:_____

_____

_____

_____

_____

_____

_____

_____

_____

_____

Verses Selected _____ _Date_____

1. I am using the following two translations:_____

_____

2. Here is my paraphrase of the passage:_____

_____

_____

_____

_____

_____

_____

_____

_____

_____

Paraphrase

Verses Selected _____ *Date* _____

1. I am using the following two translations: _____

_____

2. Here is my paraphrase of the passage: _____

_____

_____

_____

_____

_____

_____

_____

_____

_____

_____

Verses Selected _____ *Date* _____

1. I am using the following two translations: _____

_____

2. Here is my paraphrase of the passage: _____

_____

_____

_____

_____

_____

_____

_____

_____

_____

_____

Paraphrase

Verses Selected _____ *Date* _____

1. I am using the following two translations: _____

2. Here is my paraphrase of the passage: _____

_____

_____

_____

_____

_____

_____

_____

_____

_____

Verses Selected _____ *Date* _____

1. I am using the following two translations: _____

2. Here is my paraphrase of the passage: _____

_____

_____

_____

_____

_____

_____

_____

_____

_____

Paraphrase

Verses Selected _____ *Date* _____

1. I am using the following two translations: _____

_____

2. Here is my paraphrase of the passage: _____

_____

_____

_____

_____

_____

_____

_____

_____

_____

Verses Selected _____ *Date* _____

1. I am using the following two translations: _____

_____

2. Here is my paraphrase of the passage: _____

_____

_____

_____

_____

_____

_____

_____

_____

Paraphrase

Verses Selected _____ *Date*_____

1. I am using the following two translations: _____

_____

2. Here is my paraphrase of the passage:_____

_____

_____

_____

_____

_____

_____

_____

_____

_____

Verses Selected _____ *Date*_____

1. I am using the following two translations: _____

_____

2. Here is my paraphrase of the passage:_____

_____

_____

_____

_____

_____

_____

_____

_____

_____

Paraphrase

Verses Selected _____ _Date_ _____

1. I am using the following two translations: _____

_____

2. Here is my paraphrase of the passage: _____

_____

_____

_____

_____

_____

_____

_____

_____

_____

Verses Selected _____ _Date_ _____

1. I am using the following two translations: _____

_____

2. Here is my paraphrase of the passage: _____

_____

_____

_____

_____

_____

_____

_____

_____

Law Study

15 minutes

Passage Selected _____ *Date* _____

1. What does the passage command to be done or not to be done?

_____

_____

_____

2. Was this law aimed at a certain group (age, occupation, etc.)? _____

3. Would their need apply to me? _____

4. Has this law been done away with in some other part of Scripture?

_____

_____

_____

5. What is God's unchangeable principle behind this law? _____

_____

_____

_____

_____

6. Are there any passages in the New Testament which teach this
   principle? (Use cross-references) _____

_____

_____

_____

_____

7. What has God taught me for practical living from this passage? _____

_____

_____

_____

_____

120

Law Study

Passage Selected _____ *Date*_____

1. What does the passage command to be done or not to be done?

_____

_____

_____

2. Was this law aimed at a certain group (age, occupation, etc.)?_____

_____

3. Would their need apply to me?____ _____

4. Has this law been done away with in some other part of Scripture?

_____

_____

_____

5. What is God's unchangeable principle behind this law?_____

_____

_____

_____

_____

6. Are there any passages in the New Testament which teach this
   principle? (Use cross-references) _____

_____

_____

_____

_____

7. What has God taught me for practical living from this passage?_____

_____

_____

_____

_____

Law Study

Passage Selected _____ _Date_____

1. What does the passage command to be done or not to be done?

_____

_____

_____

2. Was this law aimed at a certain group (age, occupation, etc.)?_____

3. Would their need apply to me?_____

4. Has this law been done away with in some other part of Scripture?

_____

_____

_____

5. What is God's unchangeable principle behind this law?_____

_____

_____

_____

6. Are there any passages in the New Testament which teach this
   principle? (Use cross-references) _____

_____

_____

_____

_____

7. What has God taught me for practical living from this passage?_____

_____

_____

_____

_____

Passage Selected _____ _Date_ _____

1. What does the passage command to be done or not to be done?

_____

_____

_____

2. Was this law aimed at a certain group (age, occupation, etc.)? _____

_____

3. Would their need apply to me? _____

4. Has this law been done away with in some other part of Scripture?

_____

_____

_____

5. What is God's unchangeable principle behind this law? _____

_____

_____

_____

6. Are there any passages in the New Testament which teach this principle? (Use cross-references) _____

_____

_____

_____

7. What has God taught me for practical living from this passage? _____

_____

_____

_____

Law Study

Passage Selected _____ _Date_____

1. What does the passage command to be done or not to be done?

_____

_____

_____

2. Was this law aimed at a certain group (age, occupation, etc.)?_____

_____

3. Would their need apply to me?_____

4. Has this law been done away with in some other part of Scripture?

_____

_____

5. What is God's unchangeable principle behind this law?_____

_____

_____

_____

6. Are there any passages in the New Testament which teach this
principle? (Use cross-references) _____

_____

_____

_____

7. What has God taught me for practical living from this passage?_____

_____

_____

_____

_____

Law Study

Passage Selected _____ _Date_____

1. What does the passage command to be done or not to be done?

_____

_____

_____

2. Was this law aimed at a certain group (age, occupation, etc.)?_____

_____

3. Would their need apply to me?_____

4. Has this law been done away with in some other part of Scripture?

_____

_____

_____

5. What is God's unchangeable principle behind this law?_____

_____

_____

_____

_____

6. Are there any passages in the New Testament which teach this
   principle? (Use cross-references) _____

_____

_____

_____

7. What has God taught me for practical living from this passage?_____

_____

_____

_____

Law Study

Passage Selected _____ *Date* _____

1. What does the passage command to be done or not to be done?

_____

_____

_____

2. Was this law aimed at a certain group (age, occupation, etc.)? _____

3. Would their need apply to me? _____

4. Has this law been done away with in some other part of Scripture?

_____

_____

_____

5. What is God's unchangeable principle behind this law? _____

_____

_____

_____

_____

6. Are there any passages in the New Testament which teach this principle? (Use cross-references) _____

_____

_____

_____

_____

7. What has God taught me for practical living from this passage? _____

_____

_____

_____

_____

Law Study

Passage Selected _____ _Date_____

1. What does the passage command to be done or not to be done?

_____

_____

2. Was this law aimed at a certain group (age, occupation, etc.)?_____

3. Would their need apply to me?_____

4. Has this law been done away with in some other part of Scripture?

_____

_____

_____

5. What is God's unchangeable principle behind this law?_____

_____

_____

_____

6. Are there any passages in the New Testament which teach this
   principle? (Use cross-references) _____

_____

_____

_____

7. What has God taught me for practical living from this passage?_____

_____

_____

_____

_____

Law Study

Passage Selected _____ _Date_____

_1._ What does the passage command to be done or not to be done?

_____

_____

_____

_2._ Was this law aimed at a certain group (age, occupation, etc.)?_____

_____

_3._ Would their need apply to me?_____

_4._ Has this law been done away with in some other part of Scripture?

_____

_____

_____

_5._ What is God's unchangeable principle behind this law?_____

_____

_____

_____

_6._ Are there any passages in the New Testament which teach this
principle? (Use cross-references) _____

_____

_____

_____

_7._ What has God taught me for practical living from this passage?_____

_____

_____

_____

Law Study

Passage Selected _____ _Date_____

1. What does the passage command to be done or not to be done?

_____

_____

2. Was this law aimed at a certain group (age, occupation, etc.)?_____

_____

3. Would their need apply to me?_____ _____

4. Has this law been done away with in some other part of Scripture?

_____

_____

5. What is God's unchangeable principle behind this law?_____

_____

_____

_____

6. Are there any passages in the New Testament which teach this
   principle? (Use cross-references) _____

_____

_____

_____

7. What has God taught me for practical living from this passage?_____

_____

_____

_____

Prophecy Study   15 minutes

Passage Selected _____ _Date_ _____

1. Which prophet is speaking? _____

2. Whom is he speaking to? _____

3. Why was the prophecy given? _____

   _____

   _____

4. How did the people of that day respond? _____

   _____

   _____

5. What immediate event does the prophecy foretell? _____

   _____

   _____

   _____

6. Is there a second (long range) prophecy given? _____

   _____

   _____

7. Explain how each prophecy has been fulfilled. (Give fulfillment
   references if possible.)

   a. _____

   _____

   _____

   b. _____

   _____

   _____

   _____

8. What basic principle was God teaching? _____

   _____

   _____

   _____

Prophecy Study   15 minutes

Passage Selected _____ *Date* _____

1. Which prophet is speaking? _____

2. Whom is he speaking to? _____

3. Why was the prophecy given? _____
   _____
   _____

4. How did the people of that day respond? _____
   _____
   _____

5. What immediate event does the prophecy foretell? _____
   _____
   _____
   _____

6. Is there a second (long range) prophecy given? _____
   _____
   _____

7. Explain how each prophecy has been fulfilled. (Give fulfillment
   references if possible.)

   a. _____
      _____
      _____

   b. _____
      _____
      _____
      _____

8. What basic principle was God teaching? _____
   _____
   _____
   _____

Prophecy Study

Passage Selected _____ _Date_ _____

1. Which prophet is speaking? _____

2. Whom is he speaking to? _____

3. Why was the prophecy given? _____
_____
_____

4. How did the people of that day respond? _____
_____
_____

5. What immediate event does the prophecy foretell? _____
_____
_____
_____

6. Is there a second (long range) prophecy given? _____
_____
_____

7. Explain how each prophecy has been fulfilled. (Give fulfillment references if possible.)

   a. _____
   _____
   _____

   b. _____
   _____
   _____
   _____

8. What basic principle was God teaching? _____
_____
_____
_____

Prophecy Study

Passage Selected _____ _Date_ _____

1. Which prophet is speaking? _____

2. Whom is he speaking to? _____

3. Why was the prophecy given? _____
_____
_____

4. How did the people of that day respond? _____
_____
_____

5. What immediate event does the prophecy foretell? _____
_____
_____
_____

6. Is there a second (long range) prophecy given? _____
_____
_____

7. Explain how each prophecy has been fulfilled. (Give fulfillment references if possible.)

   a. _____
   _____
   _____

   b. _____
   _____
   _____
   _____

8. What basic principle was God teaching? _____
_____
_____
_____

Prophecy Study   15 minutes

Passage Selected _____ *Date* _____

1. Which prophet is speaking? _____

2. Whom is he speaking to? _____

3. Why was the prophecy given? _____
_____
_____

4. How did the people of that day respond? _____
_____
_____

5. What immediate event does the prophecy foretell? ____
_____
_____
_____

6. Is there a second (long range) prophecy given? _____
_____
_____

7. Explain how each prophecy has been fulfilled. (Give fulfillment references if possible.)

   a. _____
   _____
   _____

   b. _____
   _____
   _____
   _____

8. What basic principle was God teaching? _____
_____
_____
_____

Prophecy Study   15 minutes

Passage Selected _____ _Date_ _____

1. Which prophet is speaking? _____

2. Whom is he speaking to? _____

3. Why was the prophecy given? _____
   _____
   _____

4. How did the people of that day respond? _____
   _____
   _____

5. What immediate event does the prophecy foretell? _____
   _____
   _____
   _____

6. Is there a second (long range) prophecy given? _____
   _____
   _____

7. Explain how each prophecy has been fulfilled. (Give fulfillment
   references if possible.)

   a. _____
      _____
      _____
      _____

   b. _____
      _____
      _____
      _____

8. What basic principle was God teaching? _____
   _____
   _____
   _____

Prophecy Study

Passage Selected _____ _Date_ _____

1. Which prophet is speaking? _____

2. Whom is he speaking to? _____

3. Why was the prophecy given? _____

_____

_____

4. How did the people of that day respond? _____

_____

_____

5. What immediate event does the prophecy foretell? _____

_____

_____

_____

6. Is there a second (long range) prophecy given? _____

_____

_____

7. Explain how each prophecy has been fulfilled. (Give fulfillment references if possible.)

   a. _____

   _____

   _____

   b. _____

   _____

   _____

   _____

8. What basic principle was God teaching? _____

_____

_____

_____

Prophecy Study

Passage Selected _____ _Date_ _____

1. Which prophet is speaking? _____

2. Whom is he speaking to? _____

3. Why was the prophecy given? _____
_____
_____

4. How did the people of that day respond? _____
_____
_____

5. What immediate event does the prophecy foretell? _____
_____
_____
_____

6. Is there a second (long range) prophecy given? _____
_____
_____

7. Explain how each prophecy has been fulfilled. (Give fulfillment references if possible.)

   a. _____
   _____
   _____

   b. _____
   _____
   _____
   _____

8. What basic principle was God teaching? _____
_____
_____

Prophecy Study

Passage Selected _____ *Date* _____

1. Which prophet is speaking? _____

2. Whom is he speaking to? _____

3. Why was the prophecy given? _____
   _____
   _____

4. How did the people of that day respond? _____
   _____
   _____

5. What immediate event does the prophecy foretell? _____
   _____
   _____
   _____

6. Is there a second (long range) prophecy given? _____
   _____
   _____

7. Explain how each prophecy has been fulfilled. (Give fulfillment references if possible.)

   a. _____
      _____
      _____

   b. _____
      _____
      _____
      _____

8. What basic principle was God teaching? _____
   _____
   _____
   _____

Prophecy Study

Passage Selected _____ _Date_ _____

1. Which prophet is speaking? _____

2. Whom is he speaking to? _____

3. Why was the prophecy given? _____

   _____

   _____

4. How did the people of that day respond? _____

   _____

   _____

5. What immediate event does the prophecy foretell? ___

   _____

   _____

   _____

6. Is there a second (long range) prophecy given? _____

   _____

   _____

7. Explain how each prophecy has been fulfilled. (Give fulfillment references if possible.)

   a. _____

   _____

   _____

   b. _____

   _____

   _____

   _____

8. What basic principle was God teaching? _____

   _____

   _____

   _____

Epistle Study

Passage Selected_____ *Date*_____

1. Check the type of passage:
   ☐ Doctrinal ☐ Instructional ☐ Personal ☐ Correctional

2. Does the author give any personal information?_____

_____

_____

3. What exhortations or commands are given?_____

_____

_____

_____

4. What good qualities are encouraged?_____

_____

_____

_____

5. What problem needed correction?_____

_____

_____

_____

6. What light does the context throw on the passage?_____

_____

_____

7. What basic doctrinal truths are taught?_____

_____

_____

_____

8. What underlying principle does God want me to learn?_____

_____

_____

_____

Epistle Study   15 minutes

Passage Selected_____ *Date*_____

1. Check the type of passage:
   ☐ Doctrinal   ☐ Instructional   ☐ Personal   ☐ Correctional

2. Does the author give any personal information?_____
   _____
   _____

3. What exhortations or commands are given?_____
   _____
   _____
   _____

4. What good qualities are encouraged?_____
   _____
   _____
   _____

5. What problem needed correction?_____
   _____
   _____
   _____

6. What light does the context throw on the passage?_____
   _____
   _____

7. What basic doctrinal truths are taught?_____
   _____
   _____
   _____

8. What underlying principle does God want me to learn?_____
   _____
   _____
   _____

Epistle Study

Passage Selected_____ *Date*_____

1. Check the type of passage:
   ☐ Doctrinal ☐ Instructional ☐ Personal ☐ Correctional

2. Does the author give any personal information?_____
   _____
   _____

3. What exhortations or commands are given?_____
   _____
   _____
   _____

4. What good qualities are encouraged?_____
   _____
   _____
   _____

5. What problem needed correction?_____
   _____
   _____
   _____

6. What light does the context throw on the passage?_____
   _____
   _____

7. What basic doctrinal truths are taught?_____
   _____
   _____
   _____

8. What underlying principle does God want me to learn?_____
   _____
   _____
   _____

Epistle Study

Passage Selected_____ *Date*_____

1. Check the type of passage:
   ☐ Doctrinal   ☐ Instructional   ☐ Personal   ☐ Correctional

2. Does the author give any personal information?_____
   _____
   _____

3. What exhortations or commands are given?_____
   _____
   _____
   _____

4. What good qualities are encouraged?_____
   _____
   _____
   _____

5. What problem needed correction?_____
   _____
   _____
   _____

6. What light does the context throw on the passage?_____
   _____
   _____

7. What basic doctrinal truths are taught?   _____
   _____
   _____
   _____

8. What underlying principle does God want me to learn?_____
   _____
   _____
   _____

Epistle Study
15 minutes

Passage Selected_____ *Date*_____

1. Check the type of passage:
   ☐ Doctrinal   ☐ Instructional   ☐ Personal   ☐ Correctional

2. Does the author give any personal information?_____
   _____
   _____

3. What exhortations or commands are given?_____
   _____
   _____
   _____

4. What good qualities are encouraged?_____
   _____
   _____
   _____

5. What problem needed correction?_____
   _____
   _____
   _____

6. What light does the context throw on the passage?_____
   _____
   _____

7. What basic doctrinal truths are taught?_____
   _____
   _____
   _____

8. What underlying principle does God want me to learn?_____
   _____
   _____
   _____

Epistle Study　　　15 minutes

Passage Selected_____ *Date*_____

1. Check the type of passage:
   ☐ Doctrinal　☐ Instructional　☐ Personal　☐ Correctional
2. Does the author give any personal information?_____
   _____
   _____

3. What exhortations or commands are given?_____
   _____
   _____
   _____

4. What good qualities are encouraged?_____
   _____
   _____
   _____

5. What problem needed correction?_____
   _____
   _____
   _____

6. What light does the context throw on the passage?_____
   _____
   _____

7. What basic doctrinal truths are taught?_____　_____
   _____
   _____
   _____

8. What underlying principle does God want me to learn?_____
   _____
   _____
   _____

Epistle Study

Passage Selected_____ *Date*_____

1. Check the type of passage:
   ☐ Doctrinal   ☐ Instructional   ☐ Personal   ☐ Correctional

2. Does the author give any personal information?_____
_____
_____

3. What exhortations or commands are given?_____
_____
_____
_____

4. What good qualities are encouraged?_____
_____
_____
_____

5. What problem needed correction?_____
_____
_____
_____

6. What light does the context throw on the passage?_____
_____
_____

7. What basic doctrinal truths are taught?_____
_____
_____
_____

8. What underlying principle does God want me to learn?_____
_____
_____
_____

Epistle Study   15 minutes

Passage Selected_____ _Date_____

1. Check the type of passage:
   ☐ Doctrinal   ☐ Instructional   ☐ Personal   ☐ Correctional

2. Does the author give any personal information?_____
_____
_____

3. What exhortations or commands are given?_____
_____
_____
_____

4. What good qualities are encouraged?_____
_____
_____
_____

5. What problem needed correction?_____
_____
_____
_____

6. What light does the context throw on the passage?_____
_____
_____

7. What basic doctrinal truths are taught?_____
_____
_____
_____

8. What underlying principle does God want me to learn?_____
_____
_____
_____

Epistle Study

Passage Selected_____ *Date*_____

1. Check the type of passage:
   ☐ Doctrinal   ☐ Instructional   ☐ Personal   ☐ Correctional

2. Does the author give any personal information?_____
   _____
   _____

3. What exhortations or commands are given?_____
   _____
   _____
   _____

4. What good qualities are encouraged?_____
   _____
   _____
   _____

5. What problem needed correction?_____
   _____
   _____
   _____

6. What light does the context throw on the passage?_____
   _____
   _____

7. What basic doctrinal truths are taught?_____
   _____
   _____
   _____

8. What underlying principle does God want me to learn?_____
   _____
   _____
   _____

Epistle Study

Passage Selected_____ *Date*_____

1. Check the type of passage:
   ☐ Doctrinal   ☐ Instructional   ☐ Personal   ☐ Correctional

2. Does the author give any personal information?_____
   _____
   _____

3. What exhortations or commands are given?_____
   _____
   _____
   _____

4. What good qualities are encouraged?_____
   _____
   _____
   _____

5. What problem needed correction?_____
   _____
   _____
   _____

6. What light does the context throw on the passage?_____
   _____
   _____

7. What basic doctrinal truths are taught?_____
   _____
   _____
   _____

8. What underlying principle does God want me to learn?_____
   _____
   _____
   _____

The Five W's

Passage Selected _____ _Date_ _____

1. Skim the passage. _____

2. WHO is involved? _____
_____
_____

3. WHEN did this event take place?
   a. Approximate date: _____
   b. Day of week: _____
   c. Hour of day: _____
   d. Relationship to some other event: _____

4. WHERE did the action take place?
   a. Country: _____
   b. Province: _____
   c. City: _____
   d. Geography: _____
   e. Building: _____

5. WHAT took place? _____
_____
_____

6. WHY did this event take place? _____
_____
_____

7. What is God teaching me in this passage? _____
_____
_____
_____
_____

The Five W's

Passage Selected_____ _Date_ _____

1. Skim the passage._____

2. WHO is involved?_____

_____

3. WHEN did this event take place?
   a. Approximate date: _____
   b. Day of week: _____
   c. Hour of day: _____
   d. Relationship to some other event: _____

4. WHERE did the action take place?
   a. Country: _____
   b. Province:___ _____
   c. City:_____
   d. Geography: _____
   e. Building: _____

5. WHAT took place?_____

_____

6. WHY did this event take place?_____

_____

7. What is God teaching me in this passage?_____

_____

_____

_____

The Five W's

Passage Selected _____ _Date_ _____

1. Skim the passage. _____

2. WHO is involved? _____

_____

3. WHEN did this event take place?

   a. Approximate date: _____

   b. Day of week: _____

   c. Hour of day: _____

   d. Relationship to some other event: _____

4. WHERE did the action take place?

   a. Country: _____

   b. Province: _____

   c. City: _____

   d. Geography: _____

   e. Building: _____

5. WHAT took place? _____

_____

_____

6. WHY did this event take place? _____

_____

_____

7. What is God teaching me in this passage? _____

_____

_____

_____

_____

The Five W's

Passage Selected _____ _Date_ _____

1. Skim the passage. _____
2. WHO is involved? _____

_____

3. WHEN did this event take place?
   a. Approximate date: _____
   b. Day of week: _____
   c. Hour of day: _____
   d. Relationship to some other event: _____
4. WHERE did the action take place?
   a. Country: _____
   b. Province: _____
   c. City: _____
   d. Geography: _____
   e. Building: _____
5. WHAT took place? _____

_____

6. WHY did this event take place? _____

_____

7. What is God teaching me in this passage? _____

_____

_____

_____

_____

The Five W's

Passage Selected _____ _Date_ _____

1. Skim the passage. _____

2. WHO is involved? _____

   _____

3. WHEN did this event take place?
   a. Approximate date: _____
   b. Day of week: _____
   c. Hour of day: _____
   d. Relationship to some other event: _____

4. WHERE did the action take place?
   a. Country: _____
   b. Province: _____
   c. City: _____
   d. Geography: _____
   e. Building: _____

5. WHAT took place? _____

   _____

6. WHY did this event take place? _____

   _____

7. What is God teaching me in this passage? _____

   _____

   _____

   _____

   _____

The Five W's

Passage Selected _____ _Date_ _____

1. Skim the passage. _____

2. WHO is involved? _____

_____

_____

3. WHEN did this event take place?

    a. Approximate date: _____

    b. Day of week: _____

    c. Hour of day: _____

    d. Relationship to some other event: _____

4. WHERE did the action take place?

    a. Country: _____

    b. Province: _____

    c. City: _____

    d. Geography: _____

    e. Building: _____

5. WHAT took place? _____

_____

_____

6. WHY did this event take place? _____

_____

_____

7. What is God teaching me in this passage? _____

_____

_____

_____

_____

The Five W's

Passage Selected_____ *Date*_____

1. Skim the passage._____

2. WHO is involved?_____

   _____

3. WHEN did this event take place?
   a. Approximate date: _____
   b. Day of week: _____
   c. Hour of day: _____
   d. Relationship to some other event: _____

4. WHERE did the action take place?
   a. Country: _____
   b. Province:_____
   c. City:_____
   d. Geography: _____
   e. Building: _____

5. WHAT took place?_____

   _____

   _____

6. WHY did this event take place?_____

   _____

   _____

7. What is God teaching me in this passage?_____

   _____

   _____

   _____

   _____

The Five W's

Passage Selected _____ _Date_ _____

1. Skim the passage. _____

2. WHO is involved? _____

   _____

   _____

3. WHEN did this event take place?

   a. Approximate date: _____

   b. Day of week: _____

   c. Hour of day: _____

   d. Relationship to some other event: _____

4. WHERE did the action take place?

   a. Country: _____

   b. Province: _____

   c. City: _____

   d. Geography: _____

   e. Building: _____

5. WHAT took place? _____

   _____

   _____

6. WHY did this event take place? _____

   _____

   _____

7. What is God teaching me in this passage? _____

   _____

   _____

   _____

   _____

The Five W's

Passage Selected_____ _Date_ _____

1. Skim the passage._____
2. WHO is involved?_____
   _____
   _____

3. WHEN did this event take place?
   a. Approximate date: _____
   b. Day of week: _____
   c. Hour of day: _____
   d. Relationship to some other event: _____

4. WHERE did the action take place?
   a. Country: _____
   b. Province:_____
   c. City: _____
   d. Geography: _____
   e. Building:_____

5. WHAT took place?_____
   _____
   _____

6. WHY did this event take place?_____
   _____
   _____

7. What is God teaching me in this passage?_____
   _____
   _____
   _____
   _____

The Five W's

Passage Selected _____ _Date_ _____

1. Skim the passage. _____
2. WHO is involved? _____
   _____

3. WHEN did this event take place?
   a. Approximate date: _____
   b. Day of week: _____
   c. Hour of day: _____
   d. Relationship to some other event: _____
4. WHERE did the action take place?
   a. Country: _____
   b. Province: _____
   c. City: _____
   d. Geography: _____
   e. Building: _____
5. WHAT took place? _____
   _____

6. WHY did this event take place? _____
   _____

7. What is God teaching me in this passage? _____
   _____
   _____
   _____

Teachings of Jesus   15 minutes

Passage Selected _____ *Date* _____

1. What parable or story is told? _____
   Summarize it: _____
   _____
   _____
   _____

2. What interpretation does Jesus give? _____
   _____
   _____
   _____

3. Does He quote from the Old Testament? _____
   What? _____
   _____

4. What does Jesus condemn? _____
   Why? _____
   _____
   _____

5. What good qualities does He encourage? _____
   _____
   _____
   _____

6. What is the basic underlying principle He is teaching? _____
   _____
   _____
   _____

7. How can I apply these teachings? _____
   _____
   _____
   _____

Teachings of Jesus   15 minutes

Passage Selected_____ _Date_____

1. What parable or story is told?_____

   Summarize it: _____
   _____
   _____
   _____

2. What interpretation does Jesus give?_____
   _____
   _____
   _____

3. Does He quote from the Old Testament?_____

   What?_____
   _____

4. What does Jesus condemn?_____

   Why?_____
   _____

5. What good qualities does He encourage?_____
   _____
   _____

6. What is the basic underlying principle He is teaching?_____
   _____
   _____

7. How can I apply these teachings?_____
   _____
   _____

Teachings of Jesus   15 minutes

Passage Selected _____ _Date_ _____

1. What parable or story is told? _____

   Summarize it: _____

   _____

   _____

   _____

2. What interpretation does Jesus give? _____

   _____

   _____

   _____

3. Does He quote from the Old Testament? _____

   What? _____

   _____

4. What does Jesus condemn? _____

   Why? _____

   _____

   _____

5. What good qualities does He encourage? _____

   _____

   _____

   _____

6. What is the basic underlying principle He is teaching? _____

   _____

   _____

   _____

7. How can I apply these teachings? _____

   _____

   _____

   _____

Teachings of Jesus   15 minutes

Passage Selected _____ _Date_ _____

1. What parable or story is told? _____
   Summarize it: _____
   _____
   _____
   _____

2. What interpretation does Jesus give? _____
   _____
   _____
   _____

3. Does He quote from the Old Testament? _____
   What? _____
   _____

4. What does Jesus condemn? _____
   Why? _____
   _____

5. What good qualities does He encourage? _____
   _____
   _____
   _____

6. What is the basic underlying principle He is teaching? _____
   _____
   _____
   _____

7. How can I apply these teachings? _____
   _____
   _____
   _____

Teachings of Jesus   15 minutes

Passage Selected _____ _Date_ _____

1. What parable or story is told? _____
   Summarize it: _____
   _____
   _____
   _____

2. What interpretation does Jesus give? _____
   _____
   _____
   _____

3. Does He quote from the Old Testament? _____
   What? _____
   _____

4. What does Jesus condemn? _____
   Why? _____
   _____
   _____

5. What good qualities does He encourage? _____
   _____
   _____
   _____

6. What is the basic underlying principle He is teaching? _____
   _____
   _____
   _____

7. How can I apply these teachings? _____
   _____
   _____
   _____

Teachings of Jesus   15 minutes

Passage Selected _____ _Date_____

1. What parable or story is told? _____

   Summarize it: _____

   _____

   _____

   _____

2. What interpretation does Jesus give? _____

   _____

   _____

   _____

3. Does He quote from the Old Testament? _____

   What? _____

   _____

4. What does Jesus condemn? _____

   Why? _____

   _____

   _____

5. What good qualities does He encourage? _____

   _____

   _____

   _____

6. What is the basic underlying principle He is teaching? _____

   _____

   _____

   _____

7. How can I apply these teachings? _____

   _____

   _____

   _____

Teachings of Jesus   15 minutes

Passage Selected _____ _Date_____

1. What parable or story is told? _____

   Summarize it: _____

   _____

   _____

   _____

2. What interpretation does Jesus give? _____

   _____

   _____

   _____

3. Does He quote from the Old Testament? _____

   What? _____

   _____

4. What does Jesus condemn? _____

   Why? _____

   _____

   _____

5. What good qualities does He encourage? _____

   _____

   _____

   _____

6. What is the basic underlying principle He is teaching? _____

   _____

   _____

   _____

7. How can I apply these teachings? _____

   _____

   _____

   _____

Teachings of Jesus   15 minutes

Passage Selected _____ _Date_ _____

1. What parable or story is told? _____
   Summarize it: _____
   _____
   _____
   _____

2. What interpretation does Jesus give? _____
   _____
   _____
   _____

3. Does He quote from the Old Testament? _____
   What? _____
   _____

4. What does Jesus condemn? _____
   Why? _____
   _____

5. What good qualities does He encourage? _____
   _____
   _____

6. What is the basic underlying principle He is teaching? ____
   _____
   _____

7. How can I apply these teachings? _____
   _____
   _____

Teachings of Jesus   15 minutes

Passage Selected _____ _Date_____

1. What parable or story is told? _____

   Summarize it: _____

   _____

   _____

   _____

2. What interpretation does Jesus give? _____

   _____

   _____

   _____

3. Does He quote from the Old Testament? _____

   What? _____

   _____

4. What does Jesus condemn? _____

   Why? _____

   _____

   _____

5. What good qualities does He encourage? _____

   _____

   _____

   _____

6. What is the basic underlying principle He is teaching? _____

   _____

   _____

   _____

7. How can I apply these teachings? _____

   _____

   _____

   _____

Teachings of Jesus — 15 minutes

Passage Selected _____ Date _____

1. What parable or story is told? _____
   Summarize it: _____
   _____
   _____
   _____

2. What interpretation does Jesus give? _____
   _____
   _____
   _____

3. Does He quote from the Old Testament? _____
   What? _____
   _____

4. What does Jesus condemn? _____
   Why? _____
   _____
   _____

5. What good qualities does He encourage? _____
   _____
   _____
   _____

6. What is the basic underlying principle He is teaching? ____
   _____
   _____
   _____

7. How can I apply these teachings? _____
   _____
   _____
   _____

Topical Study

Topic Selected_____ _Date_____

Definition:

Passage References   _Summary Dealing With Topic_

_____

_____

_____

_____

_____

_____

_____

_____

_____

_____

_____

_____

_____

_____

Obtain additional passages from a concordance and cross-references.

_1._ What basic facts does Scripture teach on this topic?_____

_____

_____

_2._ What conclusions can you come to about this topic?_____

_____

_____

_3._ What can you apply to your own life?_____

_____

_____

Topical Study

Topic Selected _____ _Date_ _____

Definition:

Passage References   _Summary Dealing With Topic_

_____

_____

_____

_____

_____

_____

_____

_____

_____

_____

_____

_____

_____

Obtain additional passages from a concordance and cross-references.

_1._ What basic facts does Scripture teach on this topic?_____

_____

_____

_2._ What conclusions can you come to about this topic?_____

_____

_____

_3._ What can you apply to your own life?_____

_____

_____

Topical Study

Topic Selected _____ _Date_ _____

Definition:

Passage References   _Summary Dealing With Topic_

_____

_____

_____

_____

_____

_____

_____

_____

_____

_____

_____

_____

_____

Obtain additional passages from a concordance and cross-references.

_1._ What basic facts does Scripture teach on this topic? _____

_____

_____

_2._ What conclusions can you come to about this topic? _____

_____

_____

_3._ What can you apply to your own life? _____

_____

_____

Topical Study

Topic Selected_____ Date_____

Definition:

Passage References   *Summary Dealing With Topic*

_____

_____

_____

_____

_____

_____

_____

_____

_____

_____

_____

_____

_____

Obtain additional passages from a concordance and cross-references.

1. What basic facts does Scripture teach on this topic?_____

_____

_____

2. What conclusions can you come to about this topic?_____

_____

_____

3. What can you apply to your own life?_____

_____

_____

Topical Study

Topic Selected_____ _Date_____

Definition:

Passage References   *Summary Dealing With Topic*

_____

_____

_____

_____

_____

_____

_____

_____

_____

_____

_____

_____

_____

_____

Obtain additional passages from a concordance and cross-references.

1. What basic facts does Scripture teach on this topic?_____

_____ —

_____

2. What conclusions can you come to about this topic?_____

_____

_____

3. What can you apply to your own life?_____

_____

_____

Topical Study

Topic Selected _____ _Date_ _____

Definition:

Passage References   *Summary Dealing With Topic*

_____

_____

_____

_____

_____

_____

_____

_____

_____

_____

_____

_____

Obtain additional passages from a concordance and cross-references.

_1._ What basic facts does Scripture teach on this topic?_____

_____

_____

_2._ What conclusions can you come to about this topic?____ _____

_____

_____

_3._ What can you apply to your own life?_____

_____

_____

Topical Study

Topic Selected _____ _Date_ _____

Definition:

Passage References   _Summary Dealing With Topic_

_____

_____

_____

_____

_____

_____

_____

_____

_____

_____

_____

_____

_____

Obtain additional passages from a concordance and cross-references.

1. What basic facts does Scripture teach on this topic?_____

_____

_____

2. What conclusions can you come to about this topic?_____

_____

_____

3. What can you apply to your own life?_____

_____

_____

Topical Study

Topic Selected_____ *Date*_____

Definition:

Passage References   *Summary Dealing With Topic*

_____

_____

_____

_____

_____

_____

_____

_____

_____

_____

_____

_____

_____

_____

Obtain additional passages from a concordance and cross-references.

1. What basic facts does Scripture teach on this topic?_____

_____

_____

2. What conclusions can you come to about this topic?_____

_____

_____

3. What can you apply to your own life?_____

_____

_____

Topical Study

Topic Selected_____ *Date*_____

Definition:

Passage References   *Summary Dealing With Topic*

_____

_____

_____

_____

_____

_____

_____

_____

_____

_____

_____

_____

_____

_____

Obtain additional passages from a concordance and cross-references.

1. What basic facts does Scripture teach on this topic?_____

_____

_____

2. What conclusions can you come to about this topic?_____

_____

_____

3. What can you apply to your own life?_____

_____

_____

Topical Study

Topic Selected_____ *Date* _____

Definition:

Passage References   *Summary Dealing With Topic*

_____

_____

_____

_____

_____

_____

_____

_____

_____

_____

_____

_____

_____

_____

Obtain additional passages from a concordance and cross-references.

1. What basic facts does Scripture teach on this topic?_____

_____

_____

2. What conclusions can you come to about this topic?_____ _____

_____

_____

3. What can you apply to your own life?_____

_____

_____

Book Study

Book Selected_____ *Date*_____

BACKGROUND

1. Who is the writer?_____
   a. His occupation?_____
   b. Approximate age?_____
   c. Personality traits?_____
2. Where was the book written?_____
   _____
3. Where was it sent?_____
   _____
4. When was it written?_____
   _____
5. Why was it written?_____
   _____
   _____

THEME

1. Key thought?_____
   _____
2. Key verse?_____
3. Summary of book contents: _____
   _____
   _____

SPECIAL CHARACTERISTICS

1. What words or phrases are peculiar to this book?_____
   _____
   _____
2. What are some of its important teachings?_____
   _____
   _____

OUTLINE OF BOOK

Using a Bible Dictionary, copy the outline given for the entire book.

Main Divisions   *References*

_____

_____

_____

_____

_____

_____

_____

_____

_____

_____

_____

_____

_____

_____

_____

APPLICATION

1. Does the problem for which this book was written apply to me?____
If yes, what am I doing to correct it?___ _____

_____

_____

2. What subjects does this book deal with that I personally need?____

_____

_____

3. What different study methods will I use to study this book in greater
detail?_____

_____

Book Study   30 minutes

Book Selected_____ *Date*_____

BACKGROUND

1. Who is the writer?_____
   a. His occupation?_____
   b. Approximate age?_____
   c. Personality traits?_____
2. Where was the book written?_____
   _____
3. Where was it sent?_____
   _____
4. When was it written?_____
   _____
5. Why was it written?_____
   _____
   _____

THEME

1. Key thought?_____
   _____
2. Key verse?_____
3. Summary of book contents: _____
   _____
   _____

SPECIAL CHARACTERISTICS

1. What words or phrases are peculiar to this book?_____
   _____
   _____
2. What are some of its important teachings?_____
   _____
   _____

OUTLINE OF BOOK

Using a Bible Dictionary, copy the outline given for the entire book.

Main Divisions   *References*

_____

_____

_____

_____

_____

_____

_____

_____

_____

_____

_____

_____

_____

_____

_____

_____

_____

_____

APPLICATION

1. Does the problem for which this book was written apply to me?_____
   If yes, what am I doing to correct it?_____ _____

   _____

2. What subjects does this book deal with that I personally need?_____

   _____

3. What different study methods will I use to study this book in greater
   detail?_____

   _____

Book Study

Book Selected_____ *Date*_____

BACKGROUND

1. Who is the writer?_____

   a. His occupation?_____

   b. Approximate age?_____

   c. Personality traits?_____

2. Where was the book written?_____
_____

3. Where was it sent?_____
_____

4. When was it written?_____
_____

5. Why was it written?_____
_____
_____

THEME

1. Key thought?_____
_____

2. Key verse?_____

3. Summary of book contents: _____
_____
_____

SPECIAL CHARACTERISTICS

1. What words or phrases are peculiar to this book? _____
_____
_____

2. What are some of its important teachings?_____
_____
_____

OUTLINE OF BOOK

Using a Bible Dictionary, copy the outline given for the entire book.

Main Divisions   *References*

_____

_____

_____

_____

_____

_____

_____

_____

_____

_____

_____

_____

_____

_____

_____

APPLICATION

1. Does the problem for which this book was written apply to me?____
   If yes, what am I doing to correct it?_____ _____ __ __

   _____ _____ ____ _____ __

   _____

2. What subjects does this book deal with that I personally need?____

   _____

3. What different study methods will I use to study this book in greater
   detail?_____ _____

   _____

Book Study

Book Selected_____ *Date*_____

BACKGROUND

1. Who is the writer?_____

   a. His occupation? _____

   b. Approximate age? _____

   c. Personality traits?_____

2. Where was the book written?_____

_____

3. Where was it sent?_____

_____

4. When was it written?_____

_____

5. Why was it written?_____

_____

_____

THEME

1. Key thought?_____

_____

2. Key verse?_____

3. Summary of book contents: _____

_____

_____

SPECIAL CHARACTERISTICS

1. What words or phrases are peculiar to this book?_____

_____

_____

2. What are some of its important teachings?_____

_____

_____

OUTLINE OF BOOK

Using a Bible Dictionary, copy the outline given for the entire book.

Main Divisions   *References*

_____

_____

_____

_____

_____

_____

_____

_____

_____

_____

_____

_____

_____

_____

_____

_____

APPLICATION

1. Does the problem for which this book was written apply to me?_____
   If yes, what am I doing to correct it?_____ _____

   _____

2. What subjects does this book deal with that I personally need?_____

   _____

3. What different study methods will I use to study this book in greater
   detail?_____

Book Study

Book Selected_____ *Date*_____

BACKGROUND

1. Who is the writer?_____

   a. His occupation?_____

   b. Approximate age?_____

   c. Personality traits?_____

2. Where was the book written?_____

_____

3. Where was it sent?_____

_____

4. When was it written?_____

_____

5. Why was it written?_____

_____

_____

THEME

1. Key thought?_____

_____

2. Key verse?_____

3. Summary of book contents: _____

_____

_____

SPECIAL CHARACTERISTICS

1. What words or phrases are peculiar to this book?_____

_____

_____

2. What are some of its important teachings?_____

_____

_____

OUTLINE OF BOOK

Using a Bible Dictionary, copy the outline given for the entire book.

Main Divisions   *References*

_____

_____

_____

_____

_____

_____

_____

_____

_____

_____

_____

_____

_____

_____

_____

_____

APPLICATION

1. Does the problem for which this book was written apply to me?____
   If yes, what am I doing to correct it?_____

   _____

2. What subjects does this book deal with that I personally need?_____

   _____

3. What different study methods will I use to study this book in greater
   detail?_____

   _____